# BROKEN NEWS

# BROKEN NEWS

WHY THE MEDIA RAGE MACHINE
DIVIDES AMERICA
AND HOW TO FIGHT BACK

## CHRIS STIREWALT

CENTER
STREET®

NASHVILLE · NEW YORK

Center Street
Hachette Book Group
1290 Avenue of the Americas, New York, NY 10104
centerstreet.com
twitter.com/centerstreet

First Edition: August 2022

Center Street is a division of Hachette Book Group, Inc.

The Center Street name and logo are trademarks of Hachette Book Group, Inc.

The publisher is not responsible for websites (or their content) that are not owned by the publisher.

The Hachette Speakers Bureau provides a wide range of authors for speaking events. To find out more, go to www.hachettespeakersbureau.com or call (866) 376-6591.

Library of Congress Control Number: 2022937581

Interior book design by Timothy Shaner, NightandDayDesign.biz

ISBNs: 9781546002635 (Hardback); 9781668606391 (Audiobook); 9781546002819 (E-Book)

Printed in the United States of America

LSC-C

Printing 1, 2022

FOR JESSICA

# CONTENTS

# Introduction

# An Argle-bargle Business Model

H anging over the heads, literally, of the reporters and editors in the *Washington Post*'s newsroom on K Street are leaderboards that show which stories are clicking the best with readers in the digital world.

And what do the most active consumers of the *Post* want? Even on big news days, *Post* readers reliably plus-up stories that follow a couple of simple narratives: either wicked right-wingers getting their just deserts or the plights of innocents suffering because of right-wingers' behavior.

Even on the day of the fall of Kabul in August 2021, the biggest foreign policy story in a decade, two of the top-five most read *Post* stories according to the site's public rankings were of these kinds. One was about a Syracuse, New York, police officer suing his department for alleged racial bias, citing comments his fellow officers made about his love of gangster rap and his Tupac Shakur tattoo. But the big mover was headlined "A conservative cardinal who criticized the vaccine caught covid. Days later, he was put on a ventilator."[1]

The story about the hospitalization of seventy-three-year-old Cardinal Raymond Burke, based entirely on a press release and some old articles, was so perfect for left-wing social media that it pushed ahead of gripping stories and images from the *Post*'s own top-notch journalists on the ground in Afghanistan. The paper's tweet of the cheap, taunting Burke story got thousands of likes and retweets as well as a river of repetitive memes and cruel contempt in the comments. Gross. But so what? If bored, angry people want to go on the internet and post fake Charles Darwin quotes and argle-bargle about religion and science, it doesn't do the rest of us any harm.

Except for this: The argle-bargle is the business model.

The industry that produces the raw material out of which Americans are supposed to build political consensus is sick. The path to profitability and survival for much of the news business now relies on products that are mostly either superficial fluff or distortions that exploit and deepen our country's worsening political alienation. The hatred people feel for their fellow Americans is not just a by-product of political coverage, but a necessary component of making much of that coverage profitable.

And it's not like you don't know it. Anger at or concern about the health of the news business was for decades a mostly right-wing issue. The focus was on Republican perceptions of liberal bias in the mainstream press, so Democrats mostly shrugged off the alleged problems. The claim was consistently overblown by Republicans, but even when it wasn't, why would Democrats complain about the referees siding with the home team? But in the past twenty years—particularly since 2015 and the ascendance of right-wing populism—the worries about how the news business works have become a bipartisan obsession. As with so much today, though, partisans are talking past each other as they seek to exploit the problem for their own advantage. It is sadly fitting that the acrid, partisanship-soaked public discourse created by our dumb news media prevents needed repairs to the media itself.

My hope for this book is that we can talk about the underlying problems with the industry, not the problems as they work for or against one party or faction. This is not intended as a liberal book or a conservative book, or really a political book at all, even as it examines media and politics. I have tried in every way I can to bring a spirit of fair inquiry and impartiality to my assessments. I am sure you will find my objectivity lacking at points, but my goal here is in no way to seek partisan advantage for anyone.

As a journalist, I believe that what is wrong with my vocation and the industry in which I work is harming Americans left, right, and center. Major players in the news business are abusing their privileges and shirking their duties, and we all pay the price. There are lots of books and articles that talk about how the news media is hurting select groups: Republicans or Democrats or populists or minority groups or the family or whatever suits you. But that kind of blame casting just alienates us further, replicating the core defect of the news media that critics are attacking. There is no trophy for being *more* harmed by our lazy, alienating press. We're all losers in this one.

The agenda at many outlets is to move away from even aspirational fairness and balance and toward shared anger and the powerful emotional connections it can create. I started out talking about the problem at the *Washington Post* not because it is an industry leader in monetizing hate, but because the paper was late to the conversion to brain-dead partisan tribalism. Once famously stodgy and mainstream, the *Post* embraced a new role as a combatant in the war against Donald Trump and the American right, which created a new permission structure for what qualified as news. Journalism professor Nikki Usher praised the *Post*'s success in 2018 at using contempt to finally generate massive readership and profits. It came after the paper's long failure to cash in on angry-left rage traffic prior to the Trump era. She put it this way in an interview with NBC News: "the *Post* is optimizing for anger a little bit better."[2]

The neatest part of the "optimizing for anger" trick is that editors can let the digital newsroom leaderboards do their work for them. Reporters who want to get ahead will keep churning out simplistic, low-news-value, highly clickable stories about Tupac-loving cops or stricken old right-wing clerics. Thinking about writing something unconventional? Considering puncturing popular opinion? Want to explore political questions with subtlety and nuance? Just look up and see what the tote board says. Those aren't the kinds of stories with upward mobility.

The *Post* employs lots of top-notch reporters, some of whom are left alone to do prestige journalism, but the trend is clear: Sneering at the right and flattering the left is the house brand at the *WaPo*. That's what clicks, and it would take an iron will or a serious lack of ambition to resist. And it paid off, at least in the short term. Once the *Post* got good at chasing rage clicks, it was on its way to serious profits after years of lagging the pack. The paper would rake in more than $100 million in digital ad revenue in 2017, plus the subscriptions of more than three million digital-only subscribers.[3]

The *Post*, like many in the mainstream, is replicating a kind of coverage that was typically more common on the right at the turn of the century. Talk radio, the conservative side of the internet, and the Fox News prime-time lineup had long ago figured out the value of performative outrage and resentment. Rush Limbaugh for hours on end could lambaste the corruption, incompetence, and deceit of Democrats and the "drive-by media" without ever having to say anything bad about a Republican, unless it was to very occasionally single out the occasional "RINO." We are smart, they are dumb. We are good, they are bad. The one-sided, grievance-driven outrage made Limbaugh and some of his many imitators across right-wing media very rich.

Democrats tried to build their own left-wing echo chambers of anger, but it didn't seem to work, like Air America and the *Huffington Post*. The process, though, was only just beginning. MSNBC's prime-time shows may have been the junior varsity compared to Fox in ratings, but the playbook was now available for everyone to follow. Balanced, thoroughly reported news is hard to do, expensive, and often boring. Tribal outrage is easy, cheap, and entertaining.

What you'll see in this book is how market pressures on the news media led decision makers at outlets high to low and left to right to embrace fear and rage as business models. After decades in a stable, mostly closed marketplace, the giants of the media business were unprepared for the challenges presented by a series of threats enabled by new technology: cable television, the internet, smartphones, and social media. Those threats both enhanced and were enhanced by dramatic changes in the way Americans thought about the news and the way they consumed it, or, very often, didn't consume it at all. Like elites in almost every story of mass disruption, the rulers of the media world ignored or minimized the problem right up until the moment they freaked out. That panic led to a series of short-term decisions that would speed and intensify the coming collapse.

We watched similar cycles in lots of sectors over the past thirty years as the very same technologies and social disruptions wrought chaos. But while the news is not superior to, say, manufacturing, retail, or entertainment, it is different in one important way: The members of my vocation are supposed to discover and share information that provides the foundation for the decisions we must make together in a free society. The American system can endure without Blockbuster Video, but not without the news.

Don't worry, I'm not about to give a lecture about the First Amendment and how ours is the only industry mentioned by name in the Bill of Rights . . . something, something . . . Democracy dies in darkness . . . But I am saying that there are unique consequences to failures in the news business because of the centuries-old, close connection between the press and politics. Nor am I saying the news media used to be great and have only now gotten bad. This book is partly intended as a cure for the drippy nostalgia that afflicts so much of the discussion about what's wrong now.

As you'll see, we have been in serious trouble with how we get our news many times before. Those experiences should not only give us hope that we can get through the current troubles, but offer some insights on how to do it. But we do have to be clear-eyed about the fact that the problem in my business has serious implications for every American. A nation that doesn't have reliable access to impartial information is in trouble. A news business that makes its money by promoting political dysfunction and sharpening sectarian hatreds is a serious threat to our liberty, peace, and prosperity.

———————

How media companies make or, quite often, lose money is a driving force behind the many ills that Americans understandably complain about in journalism: shoddy reporting, sensationalism, a preference for conflict, and now, more than at any time in recent history, bias. As news outlets struggle to find profits after the great digital disruptions of the past two decades, the same social media pressures that did them in offer a pathway back to profits. Media scholar Andrey Miroshnichenko coined the phrase "post-journalism" to describe the trend.[4] Unable to sell large, diverse audiences to advertisers, news outlets increasingly focus on developing highly habituated users.

But to cultivate the kind of intense readers, viewers, or listeners necessary to make the addiction model profitable, media companies need consumers to have strong feelings. Fear, resentment, and anger work wonders. It helps news outlets create deep emotional connections to users not just as users of a product, but as members of the same tribe. As Miroshnichenko put it: "to relocate the gravity of their operation from news to values."

Rather than face opposition from the journalists actually making the content, sometimes the folks in the newsroom are pushing the same way. Reporters increasingly disdain the old virtues of fairness and balance as "bothsidesism," reimagining the ancient vice of bias as something honorable. Opinion pages become more homogeneous. Story selections become more predictable. Most ominously, post-journalism produces stifling groupthink inside news organizations and serious consequences for journalists who dissent. When powerful market pressures for coverage steeped in negative partisanship combine with the social pressures for conformity among journalists themselves, balance seems impossible and anger-driven coverage becomes inevitable.

What we think of as "bad news" can score like gangbusters if it is scary and anger-inducing. But news that is bad for your audience's ideological in-groups is clickbait kryptonite. In such a competitive marketplace, riling people up against the other side isn't enough. You've also got to create a safe space for consumers to plop down and contentedly contemplate ads for beet-based nutrient powders, reverse mortgages, and copper underpants. If you challenge their assumptions or suggest that their avatars in the culture war are wrong or losing, they may leave for competitors who offer more complete protection from harsh realities.

Take it from me. Despite a successful decade as the politics editor at the Fox News Channel, I got canned after very vocal and very online viewers—including the then-president of the United States—became furious when our Decision Desk was the first to project that Joe Biden would win the former GOP stronghold of Arizona in 2020. The call was the handwriting on the wall for Trump's chances, and it delighted Democrats almost as much as it infuriated MAGA land. Regardless of who won, we were proud to have beaten the competition yet again and defended the title network promos had given us as "the best in-class Decision Desk." But even in the four years since the previous presidential election, Fox viewers had become even more accustomed to flattery and less willing to hear news that challenged their expectations. Me serving up green beans to viewers who had been spoon-fed ice cream sundaes for years came as a terrible shock to their systems.

That's why I wrote this book, despite a strong personal aversion to the work of media criticism. I'm not saying that it can't sometimes be done well or that it isn't necessary, just that I think it's usually not worth the effort and risks. Media criticism has become its own rancid subculture inside the already rotten media business. Very often, partisans will retreat to media criticism when the actual issues are running against them. If you're a Democrat, it's a lot more appealing to talk about what nutty stuff Fox News hosts said about some screwup President Biden made than it is to talk about the screwup itself. Donald Trump based much of his strategy on the idea that the right-wing media would rather complain about mainstream coverage than talk about the issues of the day.

Indeed, media criticism is a great way to keep addicted consumers from straying. The message is obvious: Aren't you glad you're not like them, and are here with the other smart, virtuous people? To me, most of the policing that journalists do of each other is pointless. Nobody watching Don Lemon on CNN is saying, "Yeah, but they really made a good point about his bias yesterday on *Fox & Friends*." And essentially nobody watching *Fox & Friends* also watches Don Lemon. It's just more us-ver-sus-them pap.

Journalism about journalism never much appealed to me, and the idea of writing a book like this one had never crossed my mind. I would rather be writing about political history, as I did in my first book, or what the massive demographic changes in our country mean for the politics of the future. Heck, if I was writing what I really wanted to, we'd be talking about the regional cuisines of America, including, of course, the glories of the West Virginia hot dog. But my experience in my final years at Fox and the insane rage that greeted our *correct* call in Arizona told me that I had to slip on my hazmat suit and write about my own business.

So who am I to have a book's worth of observations and opinions about news? I claim no special expertise as an econ-omist or social psychologist to examine media consumption trends and the news industry. I have made many of the same mistakes and taken lots of the same sloppy shortcuts that I iden-tify as problems. I make no pretense that I have always been on the side of the angels in this business, but I have definitely paid my dues in it.

I got my first newspaper job when I was seventeen years old, the summer before I started college. It was at my hometown newspaper, the *Intelligencer* in Wheeling, West Virginia. I applied not out of any burning desire to be a reporter—I probably still imagined I'd be a lawyer or a politician then—but because I needed to get a job *fast*. I had plans for a delightfully misspent three months, but my father had other ideas. I suppose I thought newspapering might be a good resume builder. And at any rate, it was infinitely better than my other prospect: wearing a paper hat with a dancing hot dog on it while hawking frankfurters from a cart on Chapline Street.

But from the moment I entered that newsroom nearly thirty years ago, I was a goner. The carpet was held together with electrical tape and the circa 1975 word-processing terminals, yellow lacquered by cigarette smoke, required the delicate touch of a bomb technician to operate. The people who worked there were surly about their low pay and long hours, prone to foul language and a love of pitchers of cold beer. I was, of course, immediately in love. I had found my tribe.

I started out in the sports department, and most of what I did involved scut work, like taking down scores for the adult tennis or bowling from league officials who called in. But the first time I got to write just a little blurb about an American Legion baseball game and saw it in print, I was filled with the most amazing kind of joy. Words that I picked—was it a "dinger" or a "homer"— had been printed tens of thousands of times and delivered to the doorsteps of what seemed like the whole world. I lost interest in any other career path. As my college transcripts would prove, I spent much more time in the next four years on newspapering than I did on class work at Hampden-Sydney College in Farmville, Virginia. All-nighters to put out the college paper—all hail the *Hampden-Sydney Tiger!*—were exhilarating. All-nighters studying for exams were not.

After school it was back to West Virginia, where I was eventually able to get on with the *Charleston Daily Mail* in the capital city. There I got my real education in news. I worked my way up from covering the police beat, to the courthouse, to the statehouse, to my favorite, general assignment reporting. I could cover almost anything that interested me almost anywhere in the state—from investigations to days spent hanging out with carnival workers. Along the way, I got to be part of some big scoops and major stories, including breaking the news that ended the career of a sitting governor. I learned how good it felt to hold people in positions of power accountable. I learned how scary it was when they and their supporters came after you. I got my first death threats and my first fan mail. I interviewed my first president and got named in my first libel suit. Like I said, a real education.

But wouldn't you know it, right after I got the promotion to be the paper's political editor, the job of my dreams, with an office door that closed and two columns a week, the *Daily Mail* got bought to be strip-mined for cost savings. And what could be a better savings than a cocky young political editor? The new owners ultimately shut the paper down before they too got crushed by the black hole of free online content.

That drove me over to my first experience with television news, a consortium of stations around the state for which I was supposed to do investigative journalism, while also directing political coverage, while also producing and appearing on a public affairs talk show. It was not only a disaster, but endlessly disheartening. The men and women who work in local TV news have my undying respect. It is the hardest, most thankless work

I have seen in this industry. Ratings-obsessed managers armed with bogus advice from overpaid consultants trying to please skinflint owners by haranguing exhausted reporters is no way to do business. Local TV news is one of the few success stories in the business today, and we will explore some signs of hope for journalism in the world of live, local, and late breaking. But when family matters dictated a move to Washington, DC, I was not sorry to say good-bye to *Anchorman* land.

I was, however, very worried about how the hell I was going to make a living once I got there. I had no national credentials and no journalism degree. Fortunately, the newly launched *Washington Examiner* was staffing up for an audacious bid to start free, daily newspapers from coast to coast. I know, I know . . . But it was 2007, and nobody had an iPhone yet. Print journalism had been on the schneid for a decade or so, but maybe the answer was to fight the free internet with free tabloids. It sounded a little crazy, but I had my first son on the way and I was in a highly suggestible state. The Washington paper was going to be the flagship, and I would get to be its political editor, always my favorite gig.

What I found was another fantastic education. I got to edit and be edited by great talents with decades of Washington and big-time news experience. Stephen G. Smith, Mike Hedges, Bill Sammon, Michael Barone, Julie Mason, and other serious journalists had been lured by the promise of a newspaper expansion in an era of collapse and consolidation. My three years there were better than any graduate degree could ever be.

It also put me into a different world professionally. Things I would write would sometimes show up on the Drudge Report or big political blogs. It was thrilling to find that something I had written had generated responses, even negative ones, from famous names in the business. Here I was, editing copy of writers I had admired for years and simultaneously writing pieces that generated, please forgive me, buzz. Soon after came television punditry.

Believe me when I tell you that in those days, I would have gone on local cable access in a chicken suit to get airtime. It was clear to me that TV news was the best way to generate attention for your work and to show management that you were influential in Washington. I resolved that no hit was too weird, no time slot too early or late. Except for one interview I walked out on with the still-new Russia Today network, I eliminated my gag reflex. I knew that much of what passed for debate or discussion on TV was dumb to the point of being insipid, but I also knew that I could live with it as long as I didn't lie, say something I didn't mean, or pick fights for the sake of controversy. I ended up on everything from *The McLaughlin Group* to Comedy Central, sometimes cast by producers as the bow tie–clad conservative, sometimes as the just-the-facts newsman. I just tried to make sure that I kept the same perspective whatever the graphic said I was.

One holiday weekend, Sammon, a longtime Fox contributor, needed to get out of a hit, and fobbed me off on the bookers there as a replacement. Over the next two years, I would become a regular guest on the network's daytime shows. In those days, Fox booked lots of reporters from mainstream news outlets and made a point of trying to keep it mostly down the middle during daytime hours. The format suited me, and I found that a little humor was a great defense against getting sucked into arguments with other guests or for ducking questions when an anchor tried to push me to one side or another. When Sammon, who had left the *Examiner* to become managing editor at Fox, asked me to come aboard as politics editor, it was a perfect fit. I could continue to write and help coordinate political coverage, but at a much larger scale—including joining the sanctum sanctorum of the Decision Desk. All that, and I could step up my on-air contributions. What followed were some of the most enjoyable, rewarding years of my career to date.

If I had a question or wanted an interview, campaigns got right back to me. My on-air analysis made it into coverage at other outlets, and I found myself as a regular panelist on the network's marquee political show, *Special Report* with Bret Baier. I was on-air with the people who were my idols as a young politics nerd. I treasure the friendship that I made with the great Charles Krauthammer and the time I spent in greenroom banter with George Will. My near-daily hits with Megyn Kelly, first on her daytime show and then when she moved into prime time, were the most fun I ever had on-air. Working with her, Baier, and Chris Wallace on presidential debates and election night coverage was a rollicking good time. After six years at the network, I came into the summer of 2016 in the pink. Our work was good, and I had found a balance between writing, shaping coverage, and yapping on-air. My hit podcast with Dana Perino, *I'll Tell You What*, was the cherry on top. I was, of course, in for another education.

But this is not a book primarily about Fox News, nor about me. While I do have some observations to share about my experiences in cable news or elsewhere in the business that may illuminate our discussion, I have no interest in dirt dishing. We will certainly come back to the story of the 2020 election and my little role in it, but only as a case study. Insider accounts are usually self-serving and therefore terribly boring. Then there is the even more unbearably tedious kind of recounting from someone who took the money and notoriety they got from an institution for years, and suddenly had a road-to-Damascus moment after they got fired.

I was not blind to the harms cable news was causing the country in the years that I worked at Fox, nor many of the problems within my own company. But I was protected, comfortable, and well compensated. I worked in a bubble within the network with colleagues I adored and respected and was free to do the work I love. I easily rationalized my participation as making the product better, even as the news division kept getting steamrolled by the opinion mongers. As long as I was never asked to lie or say something I didn't believe, I could make my peace with it. Many people called me brave for standing up for our call in 2020 against the president and his mob. I was not being brave, just abiding by the deal I made with myself to try to stay normal-ish in a highly abnormal business.

I told you the short story of my work life from 1993 to 2021 not because it is important, but so you will understand the perspective I brought to this book. Those are my bona fides. By accident of the date of my birth and career choice, I got to see the newspaper business at the end of its fat and sassy days before the internet swallowed it whole. I got to watch as my employers tried and mostly failed to master the digital age. I have seen and experienced the pressures to shift "from news to values." I have worked in markets of every size, and from the most micro-local coverage to events with tens of millions of viewers. As they would say in Mingo County, I have been to the fair and I have seen the elephant.

But I do not hold myself out as an exemplar. As I say, I have many times failed to live up to the standards to which I aspire. My criticisms of individual journalists or outlets do not come as lightning bolts cast down from Olympus, but from the perspective of one who has been in their shoes. I believe my experience helped me understand the problem of our broken news business in a way that outsiders and academics do not. I have tried to use scholarly work and empirical data as the basis of my conclusions wherever possible, but this is mostly just my best guesses based on my experience and bolstered with research.

A couple of dull disclosures while we're doing mea culpas: I work as a scholar at the American Enterprise Institute, which is a wonderful place that provides me the freedom and resources to follow my passions where they lead me. It is a conservative institution in the best sense of that word. I am also a contributing editor at *The Dispatch*, which comes up in our discussion about ideas for how to turn things around in the business. I promise I would be plumping for *El Dispatcho* even if I didn't work there. I am also occasionally asked to appear on or write pieces for a wide array of news outlets. I don't know if those requests will dry up after this book describing the evils of mainstream news comes out, but I am generally pleased to go anywhere that's pretty much on the level, regardless of the ideology of their audience. I am for more conversation, not less.

---

The year 1942 was a dark one for Western civilization. Liberty, human dignity, and self-determination, which had been mostly advancing for centuries, were in retreat. America and Britain had been unable to stop the powers bent on replacing the gifts of the Enlightenment with a return to tyranny. Those powers may have been modern in their methods but they were as ancient in their aims as humankind itself. And it was a matter of more faith than hope that the forces of civilization could rally to save itself.

It was in that atmosphere that George Orwell reflected on the Spanish Civil War in a now-famous essay. Orwell had fought the fascists in Spain five years earlier and wanted to put the conflict in the context of the darkness that had followed. How had the free world been so willfully ignorant of the threat from modern, mechanized tyranny? He meditated on how the news media anesthetized decision makers and the public—particularly the ways in which popular demand for biased coverage prevented well-intentioned people of different points of view from reasoning together. That popular bias, Orwell said, would harden into recorded history and ultimately rob our civilization of the ability to see itself at all.

"I know it is the fashion to say that most of recorded history is lies anyway. I am willing to believe that history is for the most part inaccurate and biased, but what is peculiar to our own age is the abandonment of the idea that history could be truthfully written. In the past, people deliberately lied, or they unconsciously colored what they wrote, or they struggled after the truth, well knowing that they must make many mistakes; but in each case they believed that 'the facts' existed and were more or less discoverable. . . .

"The implied objective of this line of thought is a nightmare world in which the Leader, or some ruling clique, controls not only the future but the past. If the Leader says of such and such an event, 'It never happened'—well, it never happened. If he says that two and two are five—well two and two are five. This prospect frightens me much more than bombs—and after our experiences of the last few years that is not such a frivolous statement."[5]

This is intended to be a practical book, most of all. And I do not mean to say that it's 1942 all over again, and the light of the world is about to go out. Indeed, I am encouraged by the fact that so many Americans of different points of view understand the problem of division and addiction as a media profit model. My goal is to help journalists and the public they serve see the problems more clearly and become better producers and consumers of news so we can be better stewards of our freedom. In our closing chapters, we will look at some very down-to-earth things that could make my industry better, improve the national discussion, and make you better informed. But I do want us to proceed bearing in mind the warning Orwell provides us. There are real consequences to screwing up our informational ecosystem.

You really do have a say in this, too. These companies don't reward bad journalism because of political bias itself, but because it is easy and profitable. Their owners enjoy the clout that comes from the news business, but Jeff Bezos would still be selling you bubble-wrapped Chinese spatulas on Amazon if you didn't read the *Post*. Rupert Murdoch just as happily takes ad money for showing Spanish-language soccer matches as he does from airing Fox News opinionators warning of the immigrant menace. It's just that all the empty partisan engagement in that turbocharged geyser of feculence is too valuable for them to pass up.

There's large and growing dissatisfaction among American news consumers with the shallow, slanted coverage that drives political division and rewards outrageous conduct. But we also have to remember that this is a demand-side problem, too. For hundreds of years, journalists worked under the assumption that what the public wanted was more information, faster and better. But once we reached the point where communication was instantaneous and the volume of information was unlimited, it turned out a lot of people just wanted superficial junk. It would be like installing a new ten-thousand-dollar range in your kitchen and your family asking for mac and cheese out of the box every night. As with our track record with lots of other areas of hyperabundance—addiction, obesity, etc.—we humans are struggling badly with unlimited information access.

Eventually we will probably figure out how to be better producers and consumers of news, as we did with changes like the ones that followed radio and television. But why risk it? We can all be better citizens and neighbors to each other if we pay attention to our own media diets. Understanding different points of view means having an honest understanding of the other perspective, not a fun-house mirror version from a clickbait engineer working in a newsroom under a digital leaderboard. And it's not very interesting or fun, either. I hope this book will help you be a better news consumer not just for the sake of the republic, but so that you can be a better, happier, more optimistic, more interesting person.

# 1.

## OUT OF IDEAS
### How News Lost a Race to the Bottom with Itself

*It is not necessary to conceal anything from a public insensible to contradiction and narcotized by technological diversions.*

—NEIL POSTMAN, *AMUSING OURSELVES TO DEATH*, 1987

Real literacy is not the ability to read and write. Literacy is codebreaking.

All of us readers are deciphering: looking at abstract symbols on a screen or a page that can put a thought, an image, an idea, a feeling, even a smell, right into our heads.

*pop*

Doing that requires more than just understanding what different combinations of letters mean phonetically. You need context, culture, history, science, and philosophy to really be literate, because the code that is embedded into American English, or any language, is far more than the squiggles and sounds it represents.

If you read Robert Frost describe "easy wind and downy flake" in a snowy wood that is "lovely, dark and deep," and you

21

know about New England and farm life, you are not only taken to that place and those sensations, but to an idea about what obligations are like: "But I have promises to keep, and miles to go before I sleep."[1]

You hear the little wind puffing through the bare branches, you see the big snowflakes melting on the sleeve of your coat, you smell the horse dander, you think about how the tension between pleasure and duty can be satisfying.

If you don't know the context, though, then who cares about some creepy guy in the woods? He doesn't even have a car. The letters, words, their sounds and their definitions, are not enough. But if you have the right furnishings in your mind, Frost's 108-word poem is packed with sensations, emotions, and a big concept. He has sent you a feeling and an idea from ninety-nine years ago, and you have decoded it. But *your* version of it. Yours is different from Frost's and from mine, because we have seen different woods and known different horses.

What about a painting of a farmer and his horse in a snowy wood? Still somewhat the same idea: The artist is using shared experiences and knowledge to pull feelings and sensations out of you. But there is a little less of you in it. The painter, even an impressionistic one, has had to make some decisions for you that Frost did not. Something else is lost, too. The idea about obligations may still be there, but much fainter, much more subjective. The emotional response may be even stronger with a painting, but the concept of the traveler's sense of duty becomes weaker.

What about a photograph, though? Or a video?

Photography and videography can do the things that writing does with emotion and sense memory. A photo or a video can be taken and edited in such a way to draw out a particular response. A photographer can stage or script the subjects to convey a feeling far more potently than words alone can describe. But something is lost. Now it is *this* farmer and *that* wood. Where they were still a little abstract from the painter, here they are concrete. The horse isn't the roan you had in your mind, but a dobbin gray. The trees are aspens instead of black walnuts. You are not decoding and constructing, you are absorbing.

And the idea is obliterated. We can know with great accuracy about the physical setting—see the cold in the horse's breath, hear the wind and the harness bells—but only guess at the thoughts of the man stopping by the woods on a snowy evening. We now have a totally objective depiction but a totally subjective idea.

To say video and television are "passive media" means that they are doing most of the assembly for you, and often you do not need to bring anything but your attention. Yes, you might enjoy Bugs Bunny more in "The Rabbit of Seville" if you are familiar with Gioachino Rossini's original work, or opera in general, as Warner Bros. could more safely assume in 1950 when they put it out. But you don't need to know a libretto from a leitmotif to know that it's funny when Bugs gives Elmer Fudd a scalp massage with his toes and then turns the hunter's bald dome into a fruit salad to the bouncy, antic music Rossini wrote nearly two hundred years ago.

"Cultural literacy" is the term coined by the educator E. D. Hirsch in the 1980s to talk about the erosion in literacy already evident then from the sharp decline in SAT verbal scores among middle-class white students.[2] Even controlling for the concentrated disadvantages in some minority groups by focusing on white children of adequate means, real literacy was badly in decline forty years ago. Today it's worse. In 2020, more than half of Americans between the ages of sixteen and seventy-four read below the equivalent of a sixth-grade level.[3] Almost any fifth grader can enjoy Rossini for a rabbit, but not many can decode an abstract idea and apply it to concrete situations.

Written language is unsurpassed for the broad transmission of ideas, concepts, and philosophies. The words remain fixed and can, like the New Testament or the United States Constitution, remain in practical use for hundreds or even thousands of years. Because readers are decoding the messages for themselves, the fixity of the words is reduced as an obstacle to individual understanding. *Your* idea of a more perfect union. *Your* idea of the kingdom of God.

But it won't work if people lack the real literacy to reveal the deeper coding in the words. You could not give the Bill of Rights or the letters of the Apostle Paul to a person who knew the language phonetically and the definitions of all the words but who did not know about the ideas of the Enlightenment or the story of Jesus and expect them to understand the concepts.

Video makes far fewer demands, but can never do the same work for a society.

You can't take a picture of "liberty." You can take a picture that evokes a feeling of freedom, but not of the nature of the idea itself. You can record a video of a person acting selflessly, but not of "unconditional love."

Recordings of visual images and sounds may not be able to transmit ideas with the depth and permanence of writing, but they do offer the promise of something else useful for a society: accuracy. The recorded image can be hard evidence of what happened, not what a writer described. When Mathew Brady took his camera to the First Battle of Bull Run and showed Americans the first *objective* images of war, including its dead, he pointed to the power of the new medium to tell dispassionate truths. He pointed to news as we wish it could be: accurate in its record, undiminished by the biases of an observer, and delivered directly to the consumer. Like the name of the first great television newsmagazine: *See It Now.*

The gap, though, will not go away. Images today can show far more than the human eye can see, but they will never be able to carry the depth of code needed to maintain a civilization of ideas. As we know, literacy requires the codebook of a common culture and the ability to assemble abstract ideas in one's own mind. Video asks only that you keep your eyes on the screen. It will do almost everything else. You are a spectator, not a participant.

A citizenry in which more than half of American adults aren't literate at a level adequate to life in a free society will not be free for long. We are losing the common points of reference that allow us to discuss the abstract ideas to which our nation was built to aspire: equality, natural rights, human dignity, liberty, and self-determination. The American Creed requires written words and a common culture in which to understand them.

The news business once provided those things, albeit imperfectly. But after a struggle of more than a century to combine the accuracy of the recorded image with the deeper understanding of the written word, we find both increasingly out of reach. In their place we see subjective, politicized, emotionally manipulative coverage. We see that much of our news does not aim to make ideas understood, but to generate powerful feelings—often fear, anger, and resentment.

Those feelings do not connect the consumer to the goals of the republic or the civic life around them. Instead, the feelings become self-sufficing, forming emotional feedback loops. Looking at the news at first eases the fear of the unknown, especially the anxiety about what "the other side" is doing. But that relief quickly dissipates as the consumer is told of yet more danger and yet more wicked acts of their enemies. These draw the consumer deeper in, gorging themselves on news that affirms their negative thoughts or reinforces their feelings of superiority over members of the opposing group. There is a connection being made, but it is to the consumer's own identity group: strangers who tend to feel, look, and act as they do and who share a common enemy. And at the center of that group is the outlet itself, spinning the emotional Tilt-A-Whirl.

———————————

April 14, 1935 is still remembered as Black Sunday to some Americans who live on the Southern Plains.

For five years, an oppressive drought had gripped the land where the panhandles of Oklahoma and Texas meet the corners of Kansas, Colorado, and New Mexico, a region of 100 million acres, 500 miles by 300 miles.[4] By Palm Sunday of 1935, the hope for rain had turned to deep desperation. It was a killing kind of drought.

Settlers had flooded the region after the Homestead Act of 1862, and then Congress passed two new programs for free farmland in 1904 and 1909 that drew huge numbers of inexperienced farmers into the area.[5] That part of the country is not like the Great Plains to its northeast. The Southern Plains are rimmed by mountains, the Rockies to the west and the Ozarks and Ouachitas to the east and south. When air from the Pacific is pushed over the Rockies, it cools down and expands, releasing the moisture it had absorbed over the ocean, and then blows dry across the flat land to the east.

You can see the effects of the "rain shadow" on a topographic map in a line that falls from the eastern side of Montana and

Wyoming before it slashes south, cutting Nebraska, Kansas, Oklahoma, and Texas in half. On the west side of the line is not the deep black soil and steady rains of the Missouri and Mississippi River valleys, but a thin land and a semiarid climate.

The new arrivals' timing was good, however. Not only was the rain unusually steady, but the outbreak of the First World War created massive demand for American wheat. Eager to get in on the bonanza and without proper understanding of the weather and soil, farmers plowed up millions of acres of grassland to put in wheat.[6] Good times and rain persisted through the 1920s, so when depression and drought arrived together in 1930, the men and women of the region were unprepared for either.

The next year brought not relief, but a new menace. All of that parched land without the prairie grass to hold it down started blowing up in dust storms. As the drought persisted, the storms got worse. The drought of 1934 is said by scientists studying evidence in tree rings to have been the worst in North America in a thousand years.[7] The dust that came with it was monstrous. Mothers committed suicide, driven mad by the air that choked their children.[8] Families left behind all they had built for decades to escape the relentless, blasting grit.

Caroline Henderson and her husband had been farming in the Oklahoma Panhandle for almost thirty years when the storms began. They eventually sent their children and what remained of their livestock away, and hunkered down to try to save their farm.[9]

"In the dust-covered desolation of our No Man's Land here, wearing our shade hats, with handkerchiefs tied over our faces and vaseline in our nostrils, we have been trying to rescue our home from the wind-blown dust which penetrates wherever air can go," she wrote to a friend back in Maryland. "It is almost a hopeless task, for there is rarely a day when at some time the dust clouds do not roll over. 'Visibility' approaches zero and everything is covered again with a silt-like deposit which may vary in depth from a film to actual ripples on the kitchen floor."

By the spring of 1935, surviving these storms and enduring the drought was the sole focus of life. Even so, what happened on that Palm Sunday was beyond their imaginings. An unusual blast of cold air came ripping down from Canada. This was not the warm, gusty wind of typical dust storms, but a "norther" with high, sustained winds.[10] Residents felt the temperature drop forty degrees before the clouds of dirt came upon them. Churning black walls rising eight thousand feet in the air and hundreds of feet wide produced so much static electricity that they made their own thunder and lightning.

"Severe dust storm hit at 4:20 p.m., turning afternoon brightness immediately into midnight darkness, and absolutely zero visibility," recorded Ralph H. Guy, an observer for the National Weather Service in Kenton, Oklahoma. "It was totally dark and impossible to see without searchlight, for at least 15 minutes . . . the storm came from the north and northeast and traveled at a very great speed."[11]

That was the storm that overtook Associated Press reporter Robert Geiger and photographer Harry Eisenhard just north of Boise City, thirty-five miles away. Geiger recalled racing in front of the storm at 60 miles per hour before it finally overtook their car. It took them two hours to cover the remaining six miles, driving with the door open so they could see the edge of the highway. As word spread of Black Sunday's devastation, Geiger's account ricocheted across the country, including this line: "Three little words achingly familiar on a Western farmer's tongue, rule life in the dust bowl of the continent—if it rains."[12]

Geiger's term, "dust bowl," coupled with Eisenhard's harrowing images of black clouds as big as mountains rising over helpless towns, allowed millions of Americans to finally grasp the torture their countrymen had been enduring. The photos gave evidence of the apocalyptic scene and Geiger's words, crafted as cleanly as a Robert Frost poem, summoned the idea of this hellish cauldron. It became the center of gravity for a year and an era when much of life as people knew it ceased to be. The earth itself seemed to be turning against the American project.

---

Geiger's words could have raced around the world even if they had been written seventy years before. After reliable transatlantic cable telegraph communication between the United States and Europe was established in 1866, the world had gotten a lot smaller for the written word.[13] Domestically, sending news by telegraph had been old hat for almost a century.

When Samuel Morse sent the first-ever news dispatch by telegraph from Washington to Baltimore in 1844 about a bill stalling (obviously) in Congress, one magazine declared "space is . . . annihilated."[14] It still took three weeks to get to California by train, so maybe "annihilated" was strong, but space was squeezed down enough that Morse could start selling the *Baltimore American* congressional updates for a penny a word.[15] By the time Geiger was working out of the Denver office of the Associated Press and giving the Dust Bowl its name, Americans were well accustomed to lightning-fast news updates and hard-charging newsmen like him. "When I started out, I was going to write the great American novel," he recalled late in life, "but I got too caught up in the action."[16]

But space had only quite recently been annihilated in Eisenhard's world. Newspapers had experimented with running reproductions of photographs fifty years earlier, but for the next twenty years only used them with great rarity. It had only been fifteen years before Black Sunday that technology had advanced enough to make newspaper photographs a regular feature.[17] But you still had to have the film and the printing press in the same place to do it. News photography had bloomed in the 1920s, but it still couldn't ride lightning like words could.

There had been disappointing experiments with transmitting photos on telephone lines before, but on New Year's Day 1935 the Associated Press inaugurated its Wirephoto service with a batch of pictures from the Tournament of Roses Parade in Pasadena, California.[18] It would have taken days to get the pictures in Midwest and East Coast newspapers before; now it was in the January 2 morning papers. It required expensive, specialized equipment to code and decode the image into electrical impulses, but it took just eight minutes to send a detailed picture across the continent.[19] That meant that a few months later, Eisenhard's photos and Geiger's words could be seen together by Americans everywhere the next day.

If you wanted to pick a moment when the truly *national* news media was born, you could argue that it was in the first half of 1935, when, for the first time, Americans in every major city could read the same stories and see the same photographs simultaneously. It certainly pointed to the national news cycle as we still know it. Seventy years earlier, it had taken more than two days for news of Abraham Lincoln's death to reach even some well-settled towns in California.[20] Connectivity continued to improve after the telephone's popularity exploded in the 1880s, but there still wasn't a daily national news cycle. The first transcontinental telephone call had taken place just twenty years before AP was using phone lines to send Eisenhard's ominous images from the Oklahoma Panhandle to every corner of the nation.[21]

With the telegraph, the telephone, the Associated Press, and other national wire services well in place by the 1910s, the old regional networks that had passed news items from one part of the country to another in a fashion not so different from Ben Franklin's day had finally been wiped out.[22] But not until America could have the same ideas in the written word with the same objective record transmitted in pictures everywhere at the same time could we have a true national media. The propulsive news cycle that we still feel today goes at least as far back as a couple of journalists driving through a dust storm with the doors open trying to make it to Boise City to file their report.

Space still wasn't quite annihilated yet, but it was getting pretty wispy. The delay required to write the stories, develop and transmit the photos, print the papers, and deliver them to doorsteps and newsstands across the country built in a buffer between events and individuals. A common national news market, yes. But one in which consumers were reading about events that *had* happened. In that way, it was not so different from the news business as Americans at the Founding would have understood it. The speed of transmission went from weeks to a single day, but the concept was the same.

---

Philadelphia is the real hometown of the American newspaper business.

Chicago has a great claim to that either privileged or blameworthy status with the work that went on there at the start of the twentieth century. Boomtown Chicago produced great news-papers, great reporters, and lots of experimentation. A young Carl Sandburg, disillusioned by his efforts at socialist propa-ganda, started writing for the Chicago *Day Book* in 1914. "It's a Scripps paper, takes no advertising, and therefore tells the truth," the future three-time Pulitzer Prize winner wrote a friend.[23] "Chicago, however, is unfamiliar with the truth, can not recog-nize it when it appears, so the paper is having a steady quiet growth and seems to have large destinies ahead."

Certainly, New York has the prestige and the lineage to claim the title. The *New York Post*, founded by Alexander Hamilton and edited for fifty years by America's foremost poet of his age, William Cullen Bryant, could make a claim for the title all on its own.[24] And that's *without* having to invoke the "Headless body in topless bar" front page of 1983.[25] No city could match the list of great New York newspaper alumni, including Tom Wolfe, who wrote *The Bonfire of the Vanities*, which may be the greatest novel ever written about the business.

Philadelphia has great alumni and fascinating stories to tell, though maybe not as many as New York and Chicago have. But Philly's got Ben Franklin, and Ben Franklin is the godfather of the American news business.

When Franklin was chosen as the clerk of the Pennsylva-nia Assembly at age thirty, he was already a successful newspa-perman. He bought the *Pennsylvania Gazette* when he was just twenty-three and turned it into the most widely read paper in the colony. When he was given the clerkship in 1736, in a move his progeny in the industry would envy, Franklin used the post to steer government printing contracts to his own press.[26] When he took over as Philadelphia's postmaster in 1737, Franklin used his position to get his own newspaper delivered for free. In 1753, when he was made postmaster for all thirteen colonies, he did the same thing, but from Maine to Georgia.[27]

No press baron or media mogul today could help but admire Franklin's willingness to tangle up his civic and mercantile roles. But before anyone in the business starts pounding the table for subsidies as fat as free delivery, they should remember that Franklin was actually providing a national service. (Plus, periodicals still get subsidized rates by law, despite the cost herniating the U.S. Postal Service budget every year.[28])

The Postal Service Act of 1792 may not have been the first sweetheart deal for the newspaper business in America. But the carve-out was the first one of the new federal government and Congress's first use of its Article I, Section 8 power "to establish Post Offices and post Roads." There was considerable debate over whether that meant Congress could only *designate* existing roads and post offices as official or whether Congress could summon them into being.[29] When Congress took up the question, there were about seventy-five post offices and 2,400 miles of road to serve some three million citizens of the new constitutional republic.[30] Citizens wanted faster mail and better roads, no doubt, but the debate was important not just as a question of power or expenditure or constituent services, but as one of politics.

Most of the early newspapers in the colonies had been founded by postmasters as an obvious extension of their work.[31] Towns were far apart, and there was always a demand for news. You can see how it would have made sense that the postmaster, an appointee of the Crown after all, would be the one to print up and send along an account of what was happening in his little outpost on the edge of civilization. Franklin was far from the first to slip his own broadsheet in a mailbag.

But when the main post road that ran from Boston to Williamsburg, Virginia, made it to North Carolina in 1738 and then Charleston, South Carolina, the next year, it completed a 1,300-mile stretch that King Charles II had ordered three generations before.[32] It also dramatically changed the flow of information in the colonies.

Charles was certainly enough of a rogue that he probably would have enjoyed how much trouble the eventual completion of his project would cause the German Georges who were on the British throne instead of his own Stewart line. The post road, or the King's Highway, opened up communication between discontented subjects up and down the coast. The cities were growing and commerce increasingly brought people together. But it was newspapers, most of all Franklin's, that played the key role in sharing the ideas that would produce first a revolution and then a republic.

And that was only possible because Americans of the day were highly literate people. We have to guess at what real literacy rates might have been, but evidence suggests that as many as 95 percent of residents in Massachusetts and Connecticut between 1640 and 1700 were literate. In 1731, at the age of twenty-five, Franklin—the godfather again—created the Library Company of Philadelphia with his friends. Subscribers paid forty shillings each and were able to check out books. It caught on fast and spread quickly to other colonies and up and down the social strata. Records show subscribers were allowed to pay their fees in grain, butter, and flax.[33] When post roads opened the way for the faster transmission of ideas via newspapers, those newspapers found not only eager audiences but also consumers with the real literacy necessary to wrestle with abstract ideas about power, freedom, and self-determination.

After the American Revolution, the national discussion kept growing. By 1790 there were ninety newspapers in the new republic, more than double the number there were in 1783, the final year of the war.[34] More newspapers meant more demands on post offices and roads, which was very much on the minds of members of Congress when they considered the first postal bill in 1792. They knew they were shaping political speech and public discourse as they set the rules.[35]

Franklin had died two years before, but surely he would have been pleased to see that in principle, the carve-outs he had given himself and his fellow newspaper publishers, as in Philadelphia, across the colonies, and again when he became the first postmaster general of the United States, had survived. What else would you expect from the godfather of the American newspaper business?

It was getting harder, though, to draw the line between newspapers as public service and newspapers as a commercial endeavor. Partisan funding, the driving force behind many of the new publicans, made matters even worse.

Five years out of office and resolved to follow Washington's example of withdrawing from public life after the presidency, James Madison still remained a prodigious writer of letters and a font of advice for the admiring politicians of his party. In the summer of 1822, Kentucky lieutenant governor William Barry wrote to Madison at his Virginia home, Montpelier, to brag about and seek advice for a commission Barry was leading to explore the possibility of establishing public schools in Kentucky.[36]

"A popular government without popular information, or the means of acquiring it, is but a Prologue to a Farce or a Tragedy; or perhaps both," Madison replied, laying out the stakes for the endeavor. "Knowledge will forever govern ignorance. And a people who mean to be their own Governors must arm themselves with the Power that knowledge gives."

While their correspondence was about public education, it was informed by an era of declining public discourse. The blurry lines around government advantages for newspapermen like Franklin, as well as the press freedom Madison had written into the Bill of Rights, looked different in a new era where newspapers were increasingly tools of partisan warfare. The number of newspapers was increasing rapidly, but the content was not aimed at providing a forum for debate and ideas for shared endeavors like the *Pennsylvania Gazette* had been.

President John Adams and the Federalists had pushed through the Sedition Act of 1798 to try to squelch the brutal criticisms of his government in papers backing the party Madison had cofounded with Thomas Jefferson, the Democratic-Republicans. Adams and many on his side believed that the partisan press fell outside the protections of the First Amendment because it was undermining the republic itself. "Liberty of the press and of opinion is calculated to destroy all confidence between man and man," said Federalist representative John Allen of Connecticut.[37] "It leads to the dissolution of every bond of union."

Adams's and the Federalists' efforts to regulate the press backfired, and likely contributed to his loss to Jefferson in the election of 1800. Jefferson let the law expire after he took office. While he had benefited in the election from the partisan press, Jefferson's support for free expression couldn't be doubted given his long-held stance that "liberty depends on the freedom of the press."[38] Of course, when he was the president and his administration was the one getting battered every day in pages of pro-Federalist outlets, Jefferson took a dimmer view, even if he didn't wish to abridge free expression.

"To your request of my opinion of the manner in which a newspaper should be conducted, so as to be most useful, I should answer, 'by restraining it to true facts & sound principles only,'" then-president Jefferson wrote to an aspiring publisher in 1807.[39] "Yet I fear such a paper would find few subscribers. It is a melancholy truth, that a suppression of the press could not more completely deprive the nation of its benefits, than is done by its abandoned prostitution to falsehood."

Some of Jefferson's bitterness may have been nurtured by the brutal treatment he was getting in newspapers, including for fathering children by a woman he owned as a slave.[40] But the president was right about the fact that "prostitution to falsehood" in the name of partisan advantage could do more than Adams's law to deprive America of the benefits of a free press— including the transmission of ideas to connect the people of the fast-growing republic to the concepts of the Founding, as Franklin's papers had done. Jefferson and Madison may have dreamed of systems of public education to produce a noble, enlightened citizenry, but practically they understood that high-quality news was an urgent need.

After receiving a guarantee of extraordinary freedoms of expression but also resources for disseminating their products at the Founding, the American news media spent the following three decades locked in the same kind of performative outrage, selective coverage, and tribalism that impede our ability to transmit ideas necessary for common purpose and governance today.

What broke the spell in the 1830s was the development of new printing methods that dramatically reduced the cost per edition for newspapers. The so-called penny press tabloid papers cost a fraction of what the broadsheets that preceded them demanded.[41] Penny press publishers did not have to find political patrons to underwrite costs and could target a new audience in the expanding middle class to drive circulation and broaden their appeal to advertisers.

As we've already discussed and will explore further in later chapters, technological advancements in gathering and disseminating news can bring real pain. Our stunted and imbecilic political debates today and the incapacity they produce are in part the result of the wide introduction of around-the-clock national television news and the arrival of the internet in the 1990s. Not unlike the partisan rags of the early republic, siloed outlets today have made a calculated decision to target narrow, intense audiences to sustain them in an era when profits for high-quality, general-interest news are hard to come by. And like the early nineteenth century, the outlets' dependency on those consumers today leads to capture and, as Jefferson said, "abandoned prostitution to falsehood."

But what do you do when technology delivers a new torture device like social media instead of relief like the penny press did in the 1830s or instant transmission of photographs from coast to coast a century later?

Our old guide, Robert Frost, can help us here again: "The best way out is always through."[42]

---

When the Dust Bowl was punishing the Southern Plains in 1935, it didn't seem like just nature had turned on America. Our favorite new technology was bedeviling us, too.

In 1920, KDKA in Pittsburgh became America's first commercially licensed radio station. When it broadcast the returns from that year's presidential election from the roof of the Westinghouse Electric plant, though, hardly anyone was listening at all.[43] Americans had become very familiar in the previous decade with communication by radio signals thanks to Guglielmo Marconi's wireless telegraph and its world-shrinking wonders. But the idea that a human voice or music could be sent over great distances by invisible waves must have seemed far-fetched before KDKA called the race for Warren Harding.

But when it hit, radio hit hard. The closest thing we've probably seen in our lifetimes was the adoption of smartphones after 2007. In 1920, KDKA was hollering into the void. By 1930, radio sets were in 40 percent of American households. In the next ten years, radio ownership more than doubled. Surveys in the 1930s showed Americans were tuned in for more than four hours per day on average.[44] From zero minutes to a quarter of America's waking hours in just ten years has to count as a pretty radical transformation. By the time the 1930s were over, 28 million of America's 35 million households had a radio.[45]

But this craze that had quickly turned into a way of life was concerning to some. *New York Times* correspondent Anne O'Hare McCormick in 1932 wrote about the "great unknown force" of radio and about the "dazing, almost anesthetic effect upon the mind" from consuming passive media in such great quantities.[46] This wasn't a trip to the bijou to see one of the new talking motion pictures, a temporary escape from reality at a time when reality tended to be pretty grim. Radio quickly became the soundtrack for life.

It did not take long for crooks, charlatans, swindlers, and kooks to also see the "dazing, almost anesthetic effect" and how it might make them rich and powerful.

Senator Huey Long of Louisiana, for example. The Kingfish of corruption had not been able to finagle the position of governor-for-life in the Pelican State. Term-limited, he had to go to Washington and the Senate, from whence he could still direct his machine back home through his family and loyal retainers. But he soon found that the publicity afforded him for his colorful stemwinder speeches could give him a national platform for his particular brand of populist anger.

In February 1934, NBC broadcast Long's still-famous speech, "Every Man a King," in which he proposed his "Share Our Wealth" program, which he said would achieve at once what President Franklin Roosevelt's New Deal could never obtain.[47] Long wanted to confiscate the fortunes of the wealthy and redistribute the proceeds to the tune of $5,000 per family, "enough for a home, an automobile, a radio, and the ordinary conveniences." It was the start of Long's prospective candidacy as a challenger to Roosevelt for the 1936 Democratic nomination, but also a smash hit for NBC. The network offered Long a weekly slot for his speeches, mixtures of scripture, folksy tales from home and absolute eat-the-rich demagoguery.

Long claimed in the spring of 1935 that more than seven million people had joined almost thirty thousand local Share Our Wealth clubs he was hawking on-air like a pyramid scheme for politics.[48] Radio was good to Long, so much so that he even embraced the nickname "The Kingfish" from the most popular radio show of the day, *Amos 'n' Andy*, in which the Kingfish was a shifty grifter. Long's opponents meant it as an insult, but he loved it.[49]

I don't know what would have happened in the 1936 Democratic National Convention if Long had not been killed by an assassin the previous fall on a visit back to Baton Rouge to oversee his distant empire. Long was only forty-two and growing in his power and his boldness. I am inclined to give at least some credence to what Senator Henry Allen of Kansas said about his colleague Long in February 1935. Allen said he was "disposed to laugh at" Long, but that gave him little comfort. "I was in Germany when they first began to laugh at Hitler, who is a sort of Teutonic Huey Long without Huey's mercurial disposition and mental quickness."[50]

The good thing about Long, though, was that you could see him coming. If you could see past the comic facade, Long was an obvious, even explicit threat to the American system of government. But who would have guessed that a Roman Catholic priest from Canada would be the next populist leader to make a run at sacking the constitutional order and bringing fascist techniques to our politics?

At the height of his reach before the 1936 election, Charles Coughlin, a priest in Royal Oak, Michigan, could count more than a quarter of America's adult population as listeners to his radio show, an estimated thirty million each Sunday afternoon.[51] You've no doubt heard of Coughlin and his mix of antisemitism, Catholic nationalism, and fascistic leanings. I assume every American high school student can still not escape without a section on Coughlin. It's understandable. Maybe no single individual better embodies the reality of the threat to liberal democracy in America during the 1930s.

But he's more interesting for our project because he most certainly was a product of radio. Long was already a successful politician before he became the Kingfish and ruled a medium-sized state like his own fiefdom. You can imagine how Long could have risen to power before radio, and maybe even after the arrival of television—if he got his teeth done. But Coughlin was a man of the radio age and that "dazing, almost anesthetic effect" of the medium. His voice, with a slight Irish lilt from his immigrant parents, had that aggressive rhythm of a skillful boxer working a speed bag.

He even understood the business. When CBS radio stopped selling airtime in 1931 for national broadcasts, Coughlin put together his own network of stations to air the show.[52] Plus, without national network restrictions, he could worry less about the growing political radicalism of his message. That helped him find a new audience beyond the Catholic faithful who had been his first fervent supporters. "His program is pleasantly free from that depressing species of doleful bemoaning of man's sinful nature that is so irritating to non-churchmen," wrote critic Robert Landry in *Variety* that year.[53] Other religious broadcasters had been saccharine, and other political talkers had been dry, but Coughlin offered a potent mix of social justice progressivism with bloody-minded cultural warfare.

But lest you think that this hot-tempered political priest was an empty threat, there's concrete evidence of his effect on voters. Economist Tianyi Wang was able to show through voting patterns in 1936, the formation of Nazi-allied local groups, and, later, war bond sales that Coughlin had an effect beyond what could be explained by coincidence or overlapping factors.[54] He was not just entertaining listeners, he was persuading them.

In the course of just fifteen years, radio had fundamentally remade American life—our politics, our leisure, our culture—in ways as significant as the electric light of the 1880s and the Model T of the 1910s. Indeed, much that we think of as the conquering power of television in the twentieth century was really achieved by radio in the span of a decade. It was what replaced the hearth as the focus of the family room, and provided the basis for common popular culture. Just ask the Kingfish.

And when the news went into thin air, space really had been obliterated at last. Since the days three centuries before when colonial postmasters were slipping broadsheets into mailbags; to penny press publishers installing presses on steamboats to beat the competition to the street with election results;[55] to Samuel Morse charging a penny a word for gridlock reports by telegraph; all the way up to Geiger and Eisenhard racing the black tsunami to tell the tale of the Dust Bowl, the goal was to tell readers what *had happened* as soon as possible. In the 1930s, the new standard was to tell listeners what *was happening.* This is an obvious difference, but a deceivingly powerful one.

If you know what has happened in the news, there is a cleavage between past, present, and future. A consumer could take in all that was available or all that he or she wanted and feel confident they had "read the news" until another batch arrived. But radio and eventually cable television and the internet create the sensation of having "missed the news." Each report begins with a woosh and a gong even if it is only the same warmed-over newsloaf from the hour. The number of news events had not changed, but the live connection to the coverage created the sensation of this geyser of important information that a consumer could only ever take a sip of.

The other revolution of broadcast news was one of personality. Certainly when newspapers were king, readers had favorite columnists and personalities—Mark Twain, Ida Tarbell, H. L. Mencken, William Allen White, etc.—but the actual news dispatches were usually anonymously written until the 1920s, and even then the *New York Times* and the Associated Press resisted the trend.[56] In addition to the distance in space and time that newspapers afforded, they gave readers emotional distance. Broadcast journalism absorbed that. The most famous radio report of the era was of the 1937 crash of the airship *Hinden-burg* at Lakehurst, New Jersey. To this day, Americans remember reporter Herb Morrison's anguished line, "oh, the humanity," even if they know nothing else about the event.[57] The listener is connected not to the event itself, but to the reporter's reaction to the event. It is Morrison's humanity we recall, not the carnage in the doomed airship. No longer decoding and processing the words to describe events or ideas, the news consumer is passively receiving emotional meaning.

When television put a face with the emotive voice a decade later, the transition to news as an experience rather than the acquiring of information and ideas encoded in words was nearly complete. The battle was short and decisive: TV mopped the floor with them. But then there was a twist.

---

In 1957, 70 percent of Americans in their mid-twenties read a newspaper every day, 12 points behind the most avid readers, those in their late forties. That's according to the News Media Study survey that year.[58] In many ways, this was the pinnacle for high-quality news consumption in the modern era. But it was to be short-lived.

By the mid-1970s, older Americans continued in their newspaper habits, but a sharp drop-off among Baby Boomers was under way, according to surveys by the National Opinion Research Center at the University of Chicago. While nearly three-quarters of twentysomethings in the 1950s were reading newspapers every day, two decades later the share of daily readers under thirty had fallen to 42 percent.[59] The gap between the generations became massive—a 30 point spread between the most and least avid readers. And that gap was filled—insofar as it was filled at all—with the vastly less informative product of television news.

In the 1960s and 1970s, television news consumption was stable and dominant. Research by Professor William Mayer at Northeastern University says that in that period, almost 40 percent of all households with TVs were watching the news on an average weekday evening.[60]

Mayer's research found that by 1963, television had surpassed newspapers as the primary source for the largest group of Americans. By 1983, the percentage of Americans who got their news from television *alone* pulled ahead of all newspaper use.

By the late 1980s, Boomers had grown up, but their news consumption habits had not. That 42 percent of daily newspaper readers ticked up by a point from the mid-1970s, but stalled and then declined thereafter. The trend held with their children's generation, too. Only 22 percent of consumers in their mid-twenties were reading a paper every day at the end of the print era in 2000.

But younger consumers were not migrating from print to television as newspaper readership declined over the decades. They were just dropping out. Americans who were in their twenties in 1984 were half as likely as those in their fifties to regularly watch the evening news, according to a study by the American National Election Studies group.[61] Twenty years later, the same survey found just 8 percent of twentysomethings were regular evening news consumers. There was no corresponding increase among older Americans in the same period.

Remember, almost none of this decline came from the rise of the internet. As I've already mentioned, and as we will discuss at greater length later, the internet caused massive disruptions for the business schemes of newspapers and eventually television news, but not for news consumption. Americans had given that up in large numbers all on their own.

Television news can be far more emotionally compelling than the written version, and does not come with the need for nearly as much cultural literacy or the challenge of decoding or internalizing ideas. The combination of images and recorded sound can do amazing things to change attitudes, as with the struggle for civil rights and the broadcasts that shamed white northerners into supporting the cause. But video can also lend that power of emotional manipulation to destructive causes or even just to subdue an audience—the "dazing, almost anesthetic effect upon the mind."

Television beat newspapers by offering a passive, more emotionally engaged product. But if passivity and emotional engagement are the goals, why watch the news at all? Reality TV, video games, baby duck videos on Instagram—almost anything in the entertainment world—is easier to consume and more emotionally engaging than people showing you *important* things, no matter how slickly produced or manipulative. Like worship services or education, you can't dumb it down enough to compete with things that are dumb on purpose.

We need a truly literate citizenry capable of debating the abstract ideas and concepts that our government was founded to pursue, not people who have to be soothed and coddled to make it through twenty-two minutes—plus commercials—of blow-dried fluff and phony emotional connection to consume a little bit of news. As it turns out, the soothing and coddling couldn't even keep them anyway.

# 2.

―――――

# TURNING THE TELESCOPE AROUND
## How Media Disruption Disordered
## News Judgment

*The accumulation of all powers, legislative, executive, and
judiciary, in the same hands, whether of one, a few, or many,
and whether hereditary, self-appointed, or elective, may justly
be pronounced the very definition of tyranny.*

—James Madison, *Federalist* No. 47, February 1788

Social psychologist Lee Ross was fascinated by the cognitive tics and twitches that cause humans to reach mistaken conclusions. Why do people get it wrong so often, even when their rational minds could easily avoid the same pitfalls?

People have particular trouble with making judgments about our fellow human beings. Our own lives and history reflect with maddening regularity our species' incapacity to make correct judgments about the motives and intentions of others. Wars begin, relationships end, businesses and institutions fail often because people just can't put themselves in someone else's shoes. In my own life, many of the worst encounters I have had came from a self-centered starting assumption that another person would think and feel as I did. When people don't behave as we expect them to, things can quickly sour. That's why strategy is so hard. It's not about figuring out your opponent's *best* next move, but about what your opponent will *think* would be her or his best move. As my father would cryptically intone before every fishing trip: "You've got to think like a fish."

But it is very hard for us to really see the world as other people do, let alone a lake perch, even when we know we should.

Picture yourself driving on a congested major road. Being the wonderful, selfless person that you are, you have pulled up at the end of a long line of cars to make a right turn. As you sit contemplating your goodness and vehicular virtue, a jerk comes roaring up the middle lane and cuts off the driver about to enter the merge lane and takes the turn. You're going to wait five more minutes to get there! What an SOB! What kind of car was it? Was the driver male or female? What did they look like? Were there stickers to identify their affiliations? Because wouldn't you just know that it was a . . .

A white male in a BMW with a Trump bumper sticker and plates from the neighboring state that *everybody* knows are the worst drivers? (Though this is definitely really true about Ohio and Maryland.) A woman in a Subaru with a "coexist" sticker and a kayak rack on the roof? A Hispanic male in a beat-up white pickup truck? A mom in a minivan with one of those stick figure stickers of her family and their dog? As it turns out, it doesn't matter. Your brain will probably jump to the same conclusion regardless of who was driving. The specifics are only useful for filling in the narrative. Because whoever it is, your brain will tell you "that's how *they* are."

You, thinking yourself a virtuous person, believe that the reason you have waited your turn to merge is because of your fundamental decency. You would never cut other drivers off like that, unless you had an extremely good reason: if you were desperately late for a meeting through no fault of your own, or your dog needed to get to the emergency vet, or the contractor supply was about to close and if you didn't get the part you couldn't pour the concrete until next week, or if your daughter forgot her homework and would get an F if you didn't get it to school before third period, or if you just weren't familiar with the roads on this side of town . . .

So why didn't you assume that the person cutting everyone off had just as good a reason as you would have? Why did you mutter under your breath about BMW-driving narcissists or hippies or whatever made them different from you instead of giving them the benefit of the doubt? Because people are hard-wired to see the failings of others as character defects more than as the results of circumstance.

Professor Ross was the man who gave that all-too-human trait a name: "fundamental attribution error." In a 1977 paper, Ross laid out how the "intuitive psychology" used by laypeople often runs aground on these rocky shoals.[1] Building on loads of research in the previous decade, Ross showed how people struggle to reach the right conclusions about others because they are often blinded by a deep, unconscious bias to attribute personal failings to an individual's character and group. This was part of a profound shift in the way social psychology dealt with the ancient problem of humans so often misunderstanding each other and their motives.

You see where this is going.

It doesn't take media rage merchants very much to convince their audiences that the other people watching those other channels or reading those other sites are not just wrong, but wicked.

That's what the source code in our brains tells us to begin with. The politician from your party isn't a flip-flopper, she's a pragmatist who responds to a dynamic, rapidly evolving world. But that other guy? He's just a weather vane pointing where the wind blows because that's how *they* are in that party.

Hypocrisy is nothing new in politics, and you don't need a Stanford psychology professor to tell you that people are good at making excuses for themselves and their own groups. But exploring the depth of this innate bias is important to understanding how the modern media business model works for national political news. Whatever the other side does, even if it's identical to what your side has done in the past, is not just proof to your lizard brain that they are *wrong*, but evidence that they are *bad*. It is by exploiting this powerful tendency that any day's news can be repurposed to deepen divisions and produce arbitrary strife.

In 2014, President Barack Obama kept a coffee cup in his hand as he saluted the Marines in the honor guard that greeted him stepping down from Marine One. There was a predictable freak-out in the right-wing media about Obama's disrespect for the troops.[2] But this was only a part of a longer narrative from red-team outlets that related to Obama's disdain for America and undue deference to foreign powers. Yes, the "Obama bows" meme. It was a standard of the Obama-era Drudge Report, Fox News opinion hosts, and the rest of the pack.

When Obama bowed to Saudi King Abdullah in 2009, it was "a shocking display of fealty to a foreign potentate" that spoke to his "greater respect to Islam."[3] The depth of Obama's Saudi bow was even juxtaposed with his slighter inclination for Queen Elizabeth II on the same G20 trip.[4] When Obama dipped at the waist to greet the emperor of Japan, it led one Republican pundit to wonder, "How low will the new American president go for the world's royalty?"[5] Bad salutes, shameful bowing . . . tsk, tsk, tsk. The problem, we were told, wasn't just Obama's breach of protocol; it was what it revealed about his character and feelings about his own nation. And don't even get them started about that tan suit . . .

If you don't already know, you can guess how it played when Obama's successor, Donald Trump, bowed to Saudi King Salman or botched the protocol in meeting the British royal family or saluting a North Korean general. The same outlets that had milked every drop of potential upset from Obama's lapses and held them up as reflections of deep characterological defects ignored or minimized Trump doofus moves. Meanwhile, the blue-team outlets that had ridiculed the Fox News/right-wing obsession with Obama's blunders themselves went big with Trump's mistakes, often using the opposing side's hypocrisy as a hook.[6]

All of these stories were meaningless beyond a quick mention as actual news. But as empty vessels for partisan resentment and anger, they were great. And as Ross and his fellow social psychologists have taught us, it's even easier for our siloed media because the audience does the work for them. Our brains make the connection between mistakes, even small ones, and defective character. This bad salute is because the president doesn't respect the troops. That bad salute is "common courtesy."[7] None of it mattered except for one thing: It provided more grist for our narrowcast, partisan media. Nobody gives the benefit of the doubt or acknowledges the possibility of an honest mistake. The other driver is never taking their dog to the vet or is unfamiliar with the traffic pattern. When they cut you off in the merge lane, it's because that's how *they* are.

Every day, editors and producers go hunting for any story that will either flatter their outlet's target audience or, more likely, show the fundamental inferiority or evil of the other side. They don't do this because they are bad people themselves or even necessarily aligned with the slant of the story. It's just that this kind of contempt is profitable because it is easy to trigger. To get someone to look at a story in an impartial way takes a lot of work. That's because the journalist has to not only overcome their own innate biases, but also then work to defeat the biases in their audience, starting with fundamental attribution error. And that's risky.

Let's say MSNBC or CNN had wanted to explain how Trump's faux pas on the world stage were actually innocent mistakes or a Fox News panelist defended Obama's miscues. Would audiences be more likely to hear and consider this contrary opinion, or jump right ahead to the conclusion that the pundit, anchor, or reporter was really on the other side? I can't tell you how many viewers and readers over the years have told me that I was on this side or that side, or urged me to change who I was backing. When I explain that my job is to avoid taking sides and keep my analysis as impartial as I can make it, I'm frequently met with something between skepticism and outright hostility.

Wouldn't you know it: The late, great Professor Ross can help us with that one, too.

Ross and his colleagues Robert Vallone and Mark Lepper wanted to study the degree to which personal attitudes and internal bias affected perceptions of news coverage. In a 1985 study, they asked Stanford University students to assess their own leanings when it came to the ongoing Israeli/Palestinian conflict. At the time the experiment was carried out, the issue was big news because of a recent massacre of Shiite Muslims by Christian militiamen in the Lebanese Civil War. The charge from Israel's foes was that forces from the Jewish state had either abetted or ignored the killings.[8]

After sorting the student into their self-described pro-Israel or pro-Palestinian camps, researchers then showed the subjects *identical* news reports about the massacre. Each group said that the news reports were obviously biased against their preferred group on a number of objective measures. Pro-Israeli students saw more anti-Israel content and fewer favorable mentions. Pro-Palestinian students saw more anti-Palestinian references and fewer positive mentions. Students from both groups said that an unbiased viewer would have a more negative view of the students' preferred side after watching the report. Perhaps most significantly, students in both camps said the journalists who produced the report would have given the other side a pass for doing the same things for which they had criticized the students' preferred faction.

Yeesh.

What psychologists now call "hostile media effect" has been documented in election coverage, labor disputes, immigration policy, and most definitely in sports coverage.[9] Indeed, sports coverage is kind of the template for a lot of general news coverage, especially where politics is involved (or can be dragged into the story).

I root for the West Virginia University Mountaineers and the St. Louis Cardinals and I know in my bones that whichever network is covering a game for either of my teams is absolutely in the tank for the other side. Every fawning comment about the opponent and every cruelly unfair criticism of the good guys is further proof of what I knew going in: Our guys get no respect and they never get a fair shake from the press. If the Mountaineers are the favorites, they're being held to too high a standard. If the Cardinals are the underdogs, they're not getting enough respect. I know that this is foolishness. I know about confirmation bias, the well-documented phenomenon by which we more readily see things that comport with our worldview. I know about Lee Ross's work on fundamental attribution error and the hostile media effect. Yet, there I am sitting with my sons and fuming about Kirk Herbstreit's blatant "Mountain bias" on ESPN's *College Gameday.*

But thanks to the miracles of a connected world, I can now hear coverage of my teams from the hometown feeds. I can watch the Cardinals on Bally Sports Midwest and listen as the homers in the booth at Busch Stadium sing the praises of baseball royalty. I can have the WVU game with the booming baritone of Tony Caridi cheering on every Mountaineer drive, but treating every scoring run by the opponent with the decorum that befits such a sad event. Now that I can have the coverage I want for almost every game, the national broadcasting crews sound *even more* biased to my ear than before. Since I have flattering coverage at my fingertips, even scrupulous fairness sounds like over-the-top fairness to me.

That's why it's helpful to the bottom line of news outlets to spend so much time dumping on the coverage from competitors: It's to keep their own consumers satisfied. Given how relatively little crossover there is between audiences for left-leaning and right-leaning outlets, news organizations may feel the need to remind their consumers just how bad it is out there. When contrasted with the home-team advantage for politicians of their audience's preference, the other news outlets seem even more outrageously biased. The message is so powerful because of our innate tendencies to attribute the mistakes in others to wickedness and to automatically assume even fair coverage is slanted against our side.

National political news is an especially good vehicle for triggering and exploiting these kinds of responses. The problems on the national scale can more easily be described as existential and urgent precisely because they are remote or unfamiliar to news consumers. If you ask a partisan how to solve the biggest problems they think are facing the country, you are prone to get a lot of simple answers, most of which involve the bad people on the other side stopping what they are doing. If the other people would get out of the way, we could solve the national debt/climate change/crumbling American family/transphobia/etc.

Day after day, the stories repeat on a sort of Möbius strip of horsecrap. Issues flare up because of some random news peg or sometimes just because of what people in the news business decide they want to talk about. I laugh out loud every time a reporter prefaces a question by saying "There is a lot of controversy surrounding . . ." or "There has been a lot of discussion around . . ." Yes, and very often that controversy or discussion is entirely a product of the coverage itself. But those prefaces make it seem like the reporter isn't asking a pointless question in hopes that it might generate a sound bite to perpetuate some buzz, but only responding to some public outcry.

This infinite loop of repeating issues includes some left-side favorites and some right-side favorites, almost all of which can never and will never be resolved. Take immigration, for instance. If you went by the nature of the political debate and media coverage, you would be surprised to see that year after year, Americans are fairly united on the question of what to do when it comes to immigration and the southern border. High percentages of Americans favor strict enforcement of immigration laws *and* a pathway to citizenship for most people who entered the United States illegally in the past.[10]

While the specifics would be challenging to work out, there is already enough of a broad consensus to shape a lasting policy.

Except for three things: 1) Our dumb primary system makes support for the needed compromises potentially deadly to politicians' personal ambitions on both sides. 2) If the parties solve it, they lose it as an issue with which to raise money and try to win general elections. 3) The news media values dramatic conflict above boring consensus.

The issue is always there in the hopper to put back on the converter belt when the previous story line is losing its punch. And as long as the federal government is the focus, it's easy enough to put talking heads in a box to say that there are simple solutions but that bad strangers from a different tribe are preventing progress because of their corruption or cruelty. But the same tricks just don't work on the level where Americans actually should be devoting the majority of their attention to news: close to home.

---

You probably don't need me to tell you how complete the collapse in local news has been. Unless you're lucky enough to live in one of the markets where there is still robust, competitive, aspirationally objective news coverage, you know how weak the sauce is.

Let's first revisit some of our standard caveats. Local news coverage was never perfect in America and it has often been pretty bad. Just as we have been talking about how national media outlets became prisoners of their consumer's passions and biases, the same is of course true of the parochial press. The incentives for tough coverage of important local institutions and leaders are weak, while the rewards for flattering coverage are strong. If the local medical center is the largest employer in the area and an advertiser, few editors are going to give the go-ahead on an adversarial piece unless there's anything short of dead-solid evidence of wrongdoing.

Local news should have been and should become more brave, more independent, and more reader-oriented. Lord hear our prayer. But that does not mean that imperfect local news is worse than nothing. A cop leaning on a lamppost is not as effective as one aggressively walking his or her beat, but it is better than having no police at all. And with the staggering losses in local news that we are about to explore, the hollowing out has been so deep and so broad that it has left us vulnerable to corruption and mismanagement on the local and state levels in significant, dangerous ways. But maybe you are one of the lucky ones.

Let's say you live in Kansas City, Missouri. You have the *Star*, one of the best medium-market daily newspapers. It has suffered some as it has changed hands in recent decades, but it still offers robust daily coverage and makes a point of investigative and public-accountability reporting. Plus, you have four or five daily papers in suburban communities or at the periphery of the metropolitan area, like Lawrence, Kansas, and Independence, Missouri. There are five local TV news outlets and at least two radio stations with real newsrooms. There are more than a dozen community news organizations focusing on specific parts of the metropolitan area or cultural or affinity groups, from the century-old African American–owned paper, the *Call*, to the hipster-y cultural paper, the *Pitch*. Add to that ten or so specialty magazines or outlets doing business news, restaurants, etc., and you have a lot to choose from for a metropolitan area of 2.2 million people.[11]

Of the thirty larger metropolitan areas in the country, there are several without anything like the equivalent offerings. Riverside, California's market has twice the population of Kansas City, but its main newspaper, the *Press-Enterprise*, was bought out of a bankruptcy auction in 2016 by MediaNews Group, which specializes in cutting local newsrooms in favor of more profitable regional coverage by making clusters of publications that can share resources and content. The paper has the kind of washed-out, wan sensibility that lots of you who live in medium- and small-sized communities would recognize. There are local PBS and NPR affiliates in neighboring San Bernardino, but most of the broadcast offerings are from Los Angeles. Bummer.

But if you live in Kansas City, that's Riverside's problem, right? Your politicians and business leaders are being held accountable from time to time—at least enough to create a credible fear of exposure. There's a way to spread the word about good things in your community so folks can encourage them. There's a network of outlets reinforcing a sense of community and shared local experience. It's too bad if Riverside and a lot of other smaller places don't have it so good, but that's true of a lot of things: education, health care, law enforcement, etc. Some places have a higher quality of living than others. High-quality news coverage helps encourage other virtues in communities, but it is one of them as well. And virtues are not and can never be uniformly distributed across every American community.

Fair enough. But even if you are living in a lush local news environment, you should still care about the encroaching news deserts around the country. I'll make the case in a more detailed way in a bit, but just remember that America can't function as one political entity. Our system isn't just designed to accommodate regional and local differences; localism and regionalism actually propel problem-solving on the federal level.

Problems are best solved at the closest level possible to the affected citizens. Only a relative handful of issues fit a national format. But if Americans first think of themselves politically as members of a national party and substantially ignore the important decisions being made on the local and state level, a couple of things are bound to happen: Voters' misplaced demands for action will result in increased frustration and anger and the innate human desires for meaning and belonging will attach too strongly to mostly irrelevant national political organizations. Our dwindling supply of and interest in local news are big parts of our nation's disordered political attachments.

When we talk about the decline in local news, we are mostly talking about the decline in newspapers. As we explored in the previous chapter, even as television came to dominate the media landscape, newspapers continued to provide the backbone for news. They still do today. Just look through your local newspaper's site and see how often the coverage tracks with what is on your local evening news. Part of that is the natural overlap with breaking news, but another part is that newspapers are still the assignments desk for a lot of TV news.

As I learned early in my forays into TV news, television journalism is a logistics enterprise first. If I want to write an article about something, I need a computer, a phone, and maybe a ride to go see what's going on. If I want to put something on television, I need at a minimum a very expensive camera and specialized editing software. If I want to report on the story live, I need a satellite link. And then there's the biggest practical consideration of them all: Is there something to look at? My colleagues who come from the television side of news have had to say to me so many times, "Is there sound with that?" They mean: "Hey, newspaper dummy, we can't just have the reporter on camera for two minutes talking about some boring report."

Once we tried to do a TV story about the national debt and needed a way for viewers to visualize the size of the problem. I don't believe the story ever made air, but the dozens of bags of jelly beans may have outlasted me at Fox.

TV viewers have a hard enough time consuming news in a format that is better suited to beautiful people doing entertaining things. Even the most serious, journalistically sound television reporters have to use compelling sound and images to grab and keep viewers' attention. Much of what is in print and digital news just can't make the jump. That's why the one-thousand-word story you see in a print or digital outlet becomes a ten-second reader by a news anchor. TV is great for breaking news, good for people who want a broad overview in an efficient fashion, and helpful at calling attention to issues, but it just isn't made for doing the kind of deep dives that are needed for civic hygiene.

Local TV news not only hasn't taken the kinds of punishing blows that newspapers have, but also, the past decade has been pretty good for their side of the business. In 2020, an average of almost four million Americans watched local evening news every day, with roughly the same number watching the late news, usually at 11 p.m. or 10 p.m.[12] Another 2.4 million people on average watched the local morning news. That was good enough to produce almost $20 billion in advertising revenue in 2020. Revenues have been in a slightly lower register since the post-panic recession year of 2009, but they have been stable and are projected to grow more in the next few years.[13]

A big part of what keeps local TV news afloat is all of those terrible political ads every other year. In 2020's big earning year for local news, political advertising was worth an estimated $3.2 billion to station owners.[14] Digital advertising is starting to seriously compete for political profits—jumping from less than 3 percent of total spending in the 2016 cycle to 18 percent in

2020.[15] But another way to look at it is that the digital ads are financing the TV spending. Online political ads tend to be more about raising money and mobilizing core voters, while TV ads are more often aimed at persuading voters. Advertising research firm AdImpact estimated that 75 percent of all Facebook political ads in 2020 were for fundraising.[16]

Local TV news is one of the few places to still reach a significant concentration of voters, who we know are at least somewhat likely to be civically engaged because they're watching the news instead of scrolling TikTok. It is easier than ever for campaigns to raise money, thanks to the same digital phenomena that ripped up the fabric of our news media. But they don't really know where to spend it to get as much bang for their bucks as local TV news. Being the last old media outlets standing has been very lucrative for television stations. As we will see in our closing chapters, that has led to something of a land rush to buy up stations into bigger and bigger conglomerates with the aim of replacing the failing national media organizations. But that's not great for local news, either. As you will see, there's reason to believe that local TV is about to fall down the same mine shaft that newspapers did fifteen years ago.

So when we talk about the decline in local news, we're really talking about newspapers. Without newspapers or their digital equivalents, television news and radio just can't do the kinds of work we as citizens need them to do. Other formats *include* news. Newspapers are sold *expressly for* news. More than a century of healthy profits and the development of sturdy newsroom cultures had long established papers as the principal watchdogs and chroniclers of news in every market. Print journalism is never coming back in anything like the form in which it once dominated American news consumption, but we badly need a replacement, or replacements, and soon. What has made that so hard is the fact that the collapse of the once-mighty newspaper industry was so astonishingly swift.

American newspaper advertising hit its all-time peak in 2005 with a jaw-dropping $49.4 billion in total revenue.[17] Most impressively, that was up more than $13 billion from ten years earlier. The dot-com bubble bursting and the post-9/11 downturn had slowed growth for a minute, but as the decade progressed, sales rallied powerfully.

Newspaper advertising revenue more than doubled every ten years between 1970 and 1990, so the increase of more than 50 percent from 1990 to its peak was slower, but the scale of the raw profits were titanic. The doomsayers who had been warning throughout the same period that digital competition and declining news consumption were a dire threat looked like a bunch of Chicken Littles—right up until the sky fell.

It only took until 2010, just five years, for the industry to give back the gains of the previous two decades. Ten years later, the retreat from 2005's peak was 82 percent, down to $8.8 billion. That's still a lot of money. Add in the basically stable annual revenues from subscriptions of $11.1 billion and you have a pretty big pot of cash for providing news coverage. But not in nearly as many places.[18]

In 2000, the combined weekday circulation of America's newspapers was 55.8 million. By 2018 it was 28.6 million, a decrease of almost 49 percent. That wouldn't be such a big problem if digital revenue—ads or subscriptions—had come in to significantly offset the losses. But they did not. And when the collapse started to accelerate at the end of the 20-aughts, newspapers slashed their operations to the bone.

The University of North Carolina's Hussman School of Journalism and Media report on the American News Landscape in 2020 offers some grim data points:[19]

- Between 2004 and 2020, the United States lost a quarter of its newspapers, dropping from almost 9,000 to 6,700.
- The closures included seventy dailies and more than two thousand weeklies or nondailies, often the only source of news in their communities.
- Two-thirds of America's 3,143 counties now do not have a daily newspaper. Nearly 7 percent of counties have not only no newspaper but no alternative source of credible news coverage.
- More than half of the counties without any coverage at all are in the South.

We know intuitively that it can't be good to have fewer journalists holding our local and state leaders accountable, but can we prove it? Economists and other social scientists have looked at myriad angles to try to quantify the hunch we all feel.

One study says that in areas with less coverage of the local members of the House, in addition to the expected lack of knowledge among voters about their representative, those representatives didn't work as hard in Congress and were less likely to buck their own party congressional hearings, to serve on constituency-oriented committees (perhaps), and to vote against the party line.[20] But that may also be true of most poor areas. Certainly there is a correlation between affluence and political persuadability evident from exit polls and the swing of the suburban vote from election to election. Maybe it's just that poor areas get worse representation because of a lack of competition *and* have weak news coverage.

Okay, fine. How about the story of the *Cincinnati Post*, the longtime competitor of the dominant *Cincinnati Enquirer*? In their 2011 study, researchers Sam Schulhofer-Wohl and Miguel Garrido showed that the 2007 closure of the *Post,* which had paid particular attention to the suburban communities on the Kentucky side of the Ohio River, had at least some effect on how competitive elections were.[21]

"The next year, fewer candidates ran for municipal office in the Kentucky suburbs most reliant on the *Post,* incumbents became more likely to win reelection, and voter turnout and campaign spending fell," they wrote. "These changes happened even though the *Enquirer* at least temporarily increased its coverage of the *Post*'s former strongholds. Voter turnout remained depressed through 2010, nearly three years after the *Post* closed, but the other effects diminished with time."

Kentucky was getting more Republican at the same time, so maybe there are other explanations for fewer challengers and greater ease for incumbents. But that voter participation decrease in local elections ought to give even committed skeptics pause. And there is lots and lots and lots of evidence to suggest that there is a clear correlation between less news and less voter engagement.[22] Decreased interest in local elections isn't just bad for preventing corruption and incompetence; it's expensive.

In a report for the Brookings Institution, researchers Pengjie Gao of the University of Notre Dame and Chang Lee and Dermot Murphy, both of the University of Illinois at Chicago, quantified some of the cost by looking at the cost of borrowing in cities that had experienced a newspaper closure.[23] The idea was that with less scrutiny, municipal leaders would be less careful with money, less concerned about seeking competitive rates, more inclined to steer bond business to cronies, and more likely to end up behind on their debts, and therefore having to pay a premium for bond issuance.

Yup. "Following a newspaper closure, municipal borrowing costs increase by 5 to 11 basis points, costing the municipality an additional $650,000 per issue," they wrote.

Imagine what that means to a place like Pulaski County in central Missouri, population 53,955 in the most recent census and home to part of the U.S. Army's sprawling Fort Leonard Wood.[24] It was a Route 66 city that now sits on Interstate 44 between St. Louis to the east and Springfield to the west, but not close enough to either to draw much coverage from the media outlets there. The local newspaper, the *Daily Guide*, shut down in 2018. So, who will cover the county commission, with a budget of more than $13 million, and a thirty-person sheriff's department?[25] Darrell Todd Maurina, is who. Maurina has become a minor celebrity for his Facebook-based, one-man-band coverage of Pulaski County government. He can't match what the local paper with a six-person newsroom staff could do, but locals are lucky to have him compared to other places that have no coverage at all. His idea was to go back to basics for small-town coverage, away from regional or national news and featury fluff.

"We need to go back to what was done in the late 1800s," Maurina, a former Army civilian public affairs officer, told the Associated Press, "being everywhere at every event, telling everyone what the sirens were about last night," he said.[26] Not everyone is always happy with his persistence, but as one city councilman told the AP, Maurina is "an equal opportunity agitator" who "tries to be fair, and to be honest about it."

But not every place like Pulaski County has its own Darrell Todd Maurina to remind officials that someone is making a record of their decisions and their expenditures. Knowing what we do about human nature and behavioral psychology, you would expect the scrupulousness of officials to decrease. Like the story in Plato's *Republic* of Gyges, the shepherd who found the ring that could make him invisible, even decent men and women will engage in unjust behavior to do what they think is right if they are invisible. They may not set out to be wicked, but without scrutiny, leaders cut corners to help friends, hurt foes, and do what they perceive as "good."

Are there county commissioners, sheriffs, city council members, and other officials who preside over meetings without anyone watching who always follow the rules and engage in every correct practice and disclosure? Certainly. But as the research of Gao, Lee, and Murphy for Brookings on the cost of municipal bonds tells us, the general trend is that less scrutiny means worse government. Whether that's because of corruption like our invisible shepherd friend or just simple incompetence and misfeasance that goes undetected for longer, it's still costly. One closed newspaper, even in markets where there was another competitor still standing, like Cincinnati, decreased coverage and was costly to taxpayers. Paying an extra $650,000 to issue a bond not only wastes taxpayer dollars, but, in a small community, might make the difference in a crucial improvement. News is not a luxury item.

---

I should point out here the tension between the idea of too little coverage and too much coverage. I have for years been determinedly against the idea of video cameras in Congress, certainly at least in committee hearings. I am deeply uneasy about the increasing openness at the Supreme Court to allow video coverage of proceedings. The goal of C-SPAN and our wired-for-video Congress was to increase accountability for lawmakers and bring ordinary citizens into the process. Not only have forty years of televised proceedings had only marginal success in those goals, but video cameras have introduced new problems.

Social psychologists have known about the Hawthorne effect for nearly a century. It was discovered by a team doing an efficiency study at Western Electric's Hawthorne Works in Cicero, Illinois, in 1927 to see if changes in lighting would increase productivity.[27] What they ended up proving instead was that workers who knew they were being scrutinized by the experts increased their own productivity, regardless of the lighting scheme. It has been proven repeatedly, and though the magnitude of its clinical effects are still debated, good researchers always control for its effects in experiments.[28] But in real life, there's no debate. We know that people behave differently depending on who is watching and how.

Try this thought experiment. You are going to carry the birthday cake, covered in lit candles, into the next room to place before the guest of honor. An easy task and a fun one, since you get to see if you can start "Happy Birthday" at an octave so low that others herniate themselves trying to match it. Maybe that's just me . . .

Imagine now that you know that your entrance will be captured in a photograph. Check your hair, make sure there's no telltale remnant of frosting in the corner of your mouth, and head out. You know that you won't be the focus of the photographer, but instead the birthday girl or boy will. You have to deliver the cake facing the correct direction for that one shot that you know will be saved, shared, or posted.

Now imagine that you know someone is making a video recording. The lights will probably be brighter for the sake of the footage, and you will be more visible to the other guests as you make your entrance. You will want to avoid making a derp face as you navigate the threshold and might even decide to hold your arm that's shielding the candles a little lower so as to not obscure the shot. With video, you may not be the star of the show, but records of everything you do are being made. If you goof or do something weird like, say, starting the song super-duper low, it will live forever.

You may be the master of your fate and have banished the vice of vanity from all consideration, but even the committed stoics among us can see how for most people, even in ordinary settings, knowing we're being observed can change how we act. Not just that. The method of observation can change us, too.

Will people be more or less frank in a hearing or meeting that is being recorded on video? Will people be more or less inclined to grandstanding? Will people be more or less likely to seem cooperative with members of the opposing party? Turn on almost any congressional hearing and you will have your answer. I certainly understand the argument in favor of transparency and that the people, whether it be of Pulaski County or the entire United States of America, should be able to see everything that's going on at any time. But there is a difference between transparency and accountability, and the latter is far preferable to the former.

There is so much to watch and follow in a land of 330 million people with fifty states; 3,143 counties, parishes, or equivalent jurisdictions; and 19,502 incorporated cities, towns, villages, hamlets, and other local government entities. Even if there were a way to get every meeting of every one of those entities on camera, who would watch them all?

Having full transparency would actually *decrease* accountability because important events would just get lost in the ocean of pixels. I've many times been thwarted (at least temporarily) by officials who used Freedom of Information Act rules to their advantage. If a reporter doesn't know exactly what to ask for, officials are not obliged to connect the dots for them. By the time you've broadened out your search enough to make sure to capture the emails or memos you're looking for, officials can throw in a whole haystack of other documents to turn yours into a needle. They're being transparent, but not accountable.

There is nothing exactly like the frustration of playing a game of document Battleship with an unhelpful flack. "Any emails between the secretary and the office of compliance between April and June." Miss. "Any emails between the secretary, *the deputy secretary*, and the office of compliance between April and June." Hit. "Any emails between the deputy secretary and the office of compliance related to the use of official vehicles." You sank my cabinet officer.

Video streams and document dumps can meet the definition of transparency but can actually be a hindrance to accountability. Accountability requires journalists following basic vocational standards with adequate resources and access to platforms that draw enough attention to create economic, electoral, or legal consequences for wrongdoing. Crowdsourcing accountability can certainly work in some settings, but angry mobs are blunt instruments and not useful for providing the humdrum kind of day-in-and-day-out coverage that the news is supposed to.

For all the reasons we've discussed about partisan siloing and the loss of a shared national news diet, plus some other problems we will discuss more as we look at the unhealthy relationship between the parties and news outlets, putting political proceedings on television invites politicians to perform for a larger audience and discourages the kind of decorum and consensus building necessary to make government work. Make a transcript, maybe even an audio recording. But as we have been taught over and over, from the O. J. Simpson trial to the rise of C-SPAN committee room thespians like Ted Cruz and Cory Booker, broadcasting governmental proceedings distorts them in lots of negative ways. Reporting about the proceedings is far more likely to produce the right incentives.

That's why the collapse in local news has been so damaging. For all the dangers of highly sorted, hyperpartisan national polit-ical news, there is at least enough interest to create some bound-aries for members in each party. The way the parties themselves pick candidates and enforce doctrinal standards leaves a great deal to be desired, but the two-party system still has its advan-tages. Truly national political considerations mostly can work in the red-versus-blue heuristic. If you're trying to figure out where you stand on an issue in Washington, the way the major parties have arranged themselves is a good starting place. Again, we know the problems with too much partisanship, but it's still a very useful signal.

In local news, though, questions don't tend to be nearly as ideological. Whether or not to build a new football stadium for the high school, the conduct of the police department, a proposal for using eminent domain for a retail development, an increase in robberies, or the discovery of pollution in local waterways would all intersect with citizens' ideological beliefs. But not necessar-ily the way they would nationally. Fiscally conservative residents might want a new stadium, law-and-order Republicans don't like police brutality in their own local constabulary, probusiness resi-dents may hate the idea of the government snatching up land, criminal justice reformers don't want their houses broken into, and libertarian-leaning people don't want dirty water.

In Washington, and to a lesser degree, statehouses, it's useful to talk about issues as being red or blue. But on the county or municipal level, it just doesn't work. This is especially true in our era of extremely well-sorted political geography. We live in a country where only maybe three dozen of 435 House seats are competitive—only about 8 percent of the total. The chances of real interparty conflict on the city or county level, therefore, is not great. In most places, the divisions are among members of the same party, not between the parties themselves. What people mostly want from local government is good service, efficiency, and fairness regardless of how they see themselves politically. This is in part because people know and understand the limits of local government, in turn because they see it with their own eyes. A distant federal government might be a vehicle for an ideologue's transformational agenda, but they've seen the local yokels on the town council and know better than to ask for miracles.

You need real local journalism rooted in the community, not just a national product with a local label stuck on it, to produce better outcomes for Americans living in places without vigorous coverage. That should matter to you even if you live in a place like Kansas City, where the coverage is both deep and wide. The informational impoverishment of so many places has implications far beyond the direct harms for the communities themselves.

---

We live in a union of states, not a monolithic nation-state. Our system is designed for disputes to be resolved and policies to be introduced at the most local level possible. If the town council can't handle it, the county commission may have to come in. The state may eventually have to get involved if the costs or consequences become too great. Only the biggest or most confounding problems, though, should make it to the federal government.

But that's not what one would discern from looking at Americans' media consumption. It is very easy to get national news—almost impossible to avoid, really—and very hard to find robust local news. The clear message to Americans is that the remote national capital is more important to their lives than their statehouse or city hall, when the opposite is—or at least should be—true.

The American doctrine of political subsidiarity means that the national government is a subsidiary of the state governments, which are themselves composed of county or other local governments. The flow is mostly supposed to go from the bottom to the top, not the top down. Consider the decades of savage cultural conflict that followed the Supreme Court's 1973 decision in the case of *Roe v. Wade*. The court shifted the polarity on the flow of power when it snatched the issue from the states before a consensus—really many regional consensuses—could be reached. Congress couldn't enact a law pertaining to abortion that would please both Texas and California, so how the heck were Harry Blackmun and six of his fellow justices going to sort it out themselves?

As the *Roe* decision is finally unraveling after forty turbulent years—turbulence that warped the judicial selection process and expanded still more the power of the presidency—we look back on a clear case of what goes wrong when the national government forgets to be a subsidiary of the states. States hold a variety of policies on similarly fraught issues: the death penalty, the age of consent, assisted suicide, etc. We seldom, if ever, have to discuss those issues because they are being resolved by leaders in close proximity to their constituents.

Californians might not like Texas's rules and vice versa, but that causes very little aggravation compared to what we have now with *Roe*. The status quo on abortion and several other issues is that the blue states and the red states compete for national power to try to make the whole country live like either Californians or Texans. The result is an overpowered but still ineffectual federal government and an increasingly frustrated and excitable electorate. Much of what passes for political and governmental news these days is just about amplifying that frustration and intensifying the cycle of federal bloat and bust.

Diffused power is good because it acts as a check on the tyrannical tendency of highly centralized authority, but it is also good because it allows policies to be administered in the way best suited to individuals. In a nation of 330 million souls, nearly four million square miles, and a $21 trillion economy, the belief that there could be more than a handful of one-size-fits-all national solutions must spring from naïveté and/or a desire for power. A big part of what makes America great is that we have lots of different pluribuses in our unum.

In homogeneous societies like Japan, if the mainstream fails, there isn't another ethnic, economic, geographic, or cultural group to move the nation along. Monocultures are risky in societies in the same way they are in agriculture. If you count on one crop to survive, you are unreasonably vulnerable to blight and bad weather.

So why isn't that reflected in the news and information readily available to Americans? There are lots of reasons, but market opportunity explains a lot. Having one hundred employees for a local newspaper or television station is expensive and has, by definition, a limited area in which to seek profits. The same one hundred salaries could produce national coverage that would have far greater possibilities for return on investment.

We don't know if more high-quality local news coverage would reverse America's slide toward centralized power and populist rage politics, but we certainly know weak local coverage has both contributed to and been driven by that slide. There is good news on this front, but we are still a long way from success. We will address some of the proposals and philosophies for getting there in our closing chapters, but the most important work here is educational. Getting more Americans to understand how important local news is to the health of our system is crucial.

It's easy to hate a stranger who lives in a distant part of the country. If you are a Democrat living in the Pacific Northwest, the cartoon version you see of Republicans in the South or Appalachia on the national news would easily lead you to conclude that you and they aren't just from different cultures, but different species. You might believe almost anything about them: that they want to disenfranchise black voters, have deportation police raiding the homes of otherwise law-abiding illegal immigrants, and ban birth control. If you are a Republican in the South, you might believe that Democrats in the Pacific Northwest want no election security, open borders, and the abolition of gender. Not that some small minority people in the other places want those things, but that *all* of the people there are that way.

And why not? What Fox News shows you about Seattle or what MSNBC shows you about Alabama is mostly going to reinforce your stereotypes. The reasonable conclusion based on limited information, then, would be that those strangers aren't just wrong, but bad. They are so far removed from your group, they can be safely hated without triggering too much thinking about the commonalities that connect us as Americans.

Remember the problem of fundamental attribution error: We tend to see the failures of others as the result of characteristic traits more than we should. *You know how THEY are . . .* If national media is our primary source of news, political disagreement will increasingly not take place among members of the same tribes who have shared cultures and experiences, but instead between distant, foreign entities. And because of our tendency to see errors as characterological rather than situational, we can quickly conclude that the people we think are wrong are just bad people. And who cares about being civil to a bad person? Giving the benefit of the doubt to a bad person sounds foolish.

It's harder to hate someone who lives in the same place as you, roots for the same teams as you, sits in the same traffic as you, and faces many of the same joys and challenges as you. Our local communities are the correct building blocks for a healthy national political system, but that can't happen without lots of local news consumption.

## 3.

# BUBBLE TROUBLE
## How the News Business Lost
## Contact with the Real World

*[O]ne ought to recognize that the present political chaos is connected
with the decay of language, and that one can probably bring about
some improvement by starting at the verbal end. If you simplify
your English, you are freed from the worst follies of orthodoxy.*

—George Orwell, "Politics and the English Language," 1946

For the sake of some of our left-of-center readers, let's pause here to talk about partisan and ideological bias. There's no need, of course, to convince most right-of-center readers. The liberal media bias is an article of faith for most Republicans. And while right-wingers often overstate both the quantity and consequences of bias, that is not the same as saying it doesn't exist. Europeans routinely overestimate the prevalence of gun violence and murder in the United States, for example. But the United States still has a murder rate nearly four times higher than the European Union, according to the United Nations Office on Drugs and Crime.[1] To talk sensibly about the way the

news media works (and doesn't work), let's start with some base-
lines on bias.

Is the following headline biased? "Why 'Trust Us' Is Often a
Reason Not to Trust the Government." Most certainly. But how?
Sometimes it's easy to see the presence and direction of bias just
by a headline. Consider this from right-wing site The Federalist:
"'Encanto's' Luisa Is Way Too Beefy for a Woman." The headline writer wants you to know not only that the story is biased,
but that it is biased in an antifeminist direction. By being mean
about a character in a children's movie, the headline writer also
wants to prime readers for an emotional response and, duh, a
click. That's bias and salaciousness as a business technique, and
even the capybaras in *Encanto* would know enough to discern
such obvious clickbait.

But back to "Why 'Trust Us' Is Often a Reason Not to Trust
the Government." You should know that the headline flew with
an "analysis" flag, which is a way for news outlets to say that what
follows is the work of a putatively objective reporter, but one who
is going to cut a few corners in the name of better illuminating a
subject. Or maybe just that the reporter filed a self-centered piece
of junk at deadline on a Friday and the editors figured it would
be easier to label it as ground beef than try to cut it into steaks.
News analysis really can be good and helpful. Indeed, much of
my daily writing that I like best is analysis, which lives in a gray
area between straight news and opinion. It's sort of like writing
news, but with all the adjectives switched on.

I try to avoid having opinions about what politicians or partisans *should* do, even as I offer my opinions about *how* they are
doing it. There are more than enough media mouths commenting
on what they think other people should be doing. Plus, prescrip-
tive opinions distort our ability to see things clearly. If I decree

that so-and-so should do such-and-such, I am emotionally and socially invested in the outcome. I will be less likely to see events as advantageous for the opposing side or disadvantageous for my own stated position. That prevents me from doing my favorite thing of all: figuring out what comes next. I'm always trying, and usually failing, to determine where we are politically in relation to our past and future. Hard-and-fast pronouncements are sometimes needed, but generally they make that work even more difficult. Analysis fits the bill better for the kind of work I like to do, and allows for some zhuzh in the headlines, like we saw with the one above about not trusting the government.

You've probably guessed that the headline is a misdirection play. It's from the *New York Times* on a piece venting the outrage among many journalists at the civilian casualties from American military action. It is a good thing for reporters to be skeptical of government claims about military action, but that perspective is stereotypically more left-wing than right-wing. When I see a headline or a segment about why not to trust the government, that's usually much more of a right-wing concept, often depicted in a negative, kooky way. The headline therefore works because it is interesting to see at the liberal *New York Times*—modest clickbaiting—and then takes you to a story that is about something completely different than what a reader might expect.

So is "Why 'Trust Us' Is Often a Reason Not to Trust the Government" a biased headline? Yeah, kinda. In which direction? It depends on how you look at it . . . Try putting that into a bias detection machine or scoring it in an objective way. Like most things in life, we can only try to use our best, but always imperfect, judgment. But that will never stop social scientists from trying.

A 2020 study from a group of respected political scientists claims "there is no liberal media bias in which news stories political journalists choose to cover," which is kind of a silly thing to explore.[2] Most of the stories that political journalists cover are determined by events, and most political journalists follow stories like little kids playing soccer: They form a clump and then chase the ball wherever it goes on the field.

Showing a lack of bias in "story selection," especially if one takes a capacious view of what the topic for a story is, doesn't tell us much. How those stories are written, which candidates or parties are cast positively or negatively, and which personal attributes are associated with which candidates would be far more indicative of bias. But that's too subjective for reliable, uniform research. If a dozen reporters cover a candidate debate and nine file stories saying that the Republican candidate outperformed the Democrat, is that bias, accuracy, groupthink, or something else? Some of each?

I don't mean to pick on their work, which is very well done, and, as we will soon see, parts of it are very useful. But political scientists quickly outrun their supply lines when it attacks subjective targets. Bias is a highly subjective characteristic in coverage, and social science has mostly been unable to study it empirically.

The professors' method, so you know, involved sending fictitious campaign emails to journalists. The carefully crafted spoofs invited them to sit-down interviews with state legislative candidates to see whether they responded at higher rates to campaigns of candidates of one party or another. I know I am in many ways not indicative of journalists as a whole—thank heaven for small favors—but I wouldn't participate in a sit-down interview with an unknown candidate for state legislature to see the Last

Supper with the original cast. Unless you're specifically covering the statehouse, you would run for dear life from press secretaries like those who would send such an email. Yet again, the effort to scientifically prove or disprove bias on an industry-wide scale ends up in a shrug.

But the work of political scientists Hans Hassell of Florida State University, John Holbein of the University of Virginia, and Matthew Miles of Brigham Young University is useful to our effort to be clear-eyed about bias in the press. Their study involved a massive survey of political journalists across the country that netted 1,511 responses.[3] While that was a response rate of just 13.1 percent, when you remember that the typical response rate for a high-quality national survey of the general population is typically under 10 percent these days, it doesn't seem so bad.

We should remember, though, that there's going to be considerable self-selection bias in a survey like this. We know that response rates to polls among Republicans in the larger public are below those for Democrats, so it stands to reason that the sample of journalists willing to respond to an email survey about their political leanings might also tilt left. But how far?

In the survey, nearly 8 in 10 respondents said they at least leaned toward one party. Of those who admitted a personal preference, 78 percent of respondents described themselves as liberal, and 78.2 percent described themselves as Democrats. Just 22 percent described themselves as conservative, and 21.8 percent said they were Republicans. Even if we allow for dramatically different response rates, does anyone suppose that it would cover a difference of almost fourfold? No way.

(Kudos, by the way, to the minority who said they had no partisan leanings themselves. As I've said before, that's a good thing even if some of them are deceiving themselves or the researchers. Impartiality is a good goal, even when we fail to achieve it fully.)

The researchers had another way to check their work, too. They looked at the Twitter accounts of all of the individuals on their master list—6,801 political journalists across the country—to see whom they followed. That helps control for the partisan response rate problem in an opt-in survey, for sure. But we do know that Twitter users in general tend to be younger than Americans as a whole and therefore more to the left. So, we would expect some corresponding leftward tilt among the subpopulation of journalists who are Twitter users, too. And yes, journalists on Twitter need to follow individuals with whom they don't agree, which may skew follows left, too. I don't know how much, but it certainly made me think that it would need to be a very profound kind of number in a study like that to take significant notice.

So how about these apples: "A full 78.1 percent of journalists are more liberal than the average Twitter user. Moreover, 66 percent are even more liberal than former President Obama, 62.3 percent are to the left of the median Senate Democrat (in the 114th Congress), and a full 14.5 percent are more liberal than Alexandria Ocasio-Cortez (one of the most liberal members of the House)."

Even among the left-leaning world of Twitter and even among Democrats, political journalists on Twitter are way, way left of center. Whatever the partisan response rates were to their decoy emails for statehouse candidate announcements, there's no question of the strong bent of political journalists personally to the left. All that we know about human nature and unconscious bias tells us that that has to have implications for how stories are covered. I'm not talking here about the volume or intensity or even the specific direction of the left-leaning bias, just that it exists.

If you still want some hard numbers for what is an inherently subjective measurement, though, check out the famous 2005 study "A Measure of Media Bias," by economists Tim Groseclose, now of George Mason University, and Jeff Milyo, now head of the economics department at the University of Missouri.

Groseclose and Milyo looked at the two hundred think tanks most commonly cited by major news outlets and lawmakers. They plotted ideological scores for the think tanks based on the approving mentions by members of Congress in their output of speeches and other communications. The researchers then synched that up with the lawmakers' ideological scores from the left-wing Americans for Democratic Action to generate a value on a scale of 0–100, 0 being the most conservative, 100 being the most liberal. The median score for a House member in 2003 was 39.[4]

The Heritage Foundation, then a bulwark of conservatism, got a score of 6 while the Children's Defense Fund, a close ally of Hillary Clinton, got a 77. The researchers then looked at citations of the think tanks in news reporting—not opinion pieces, letters to the editor, or editorials—at a number of major outlets from 1990 to 2003, including: the *New York Times*, *Time* magazine, *CBS Evening News*, *USA Today*, *NBC Nightly News*, ABC's *Good Morning America*, *PBS NewsHour*, the *Washington Post*, NPR's *Morning Edition*, *ABC World News Tonight*, and Fox News' *Special Report*. Groseclose and Milyo then generated a score for each show or publication.

Only *Special Report* landed to the right of the median ideological score for House members with a 27, 12 points to the conservative side of the centerline. Every other publication or show was to the left except *Good Morning America*, which back then sat smack dab on the median score of 39. The *New York Times, Time* magazine, *CBS Evening News, USA Today*, and *NBC Nightly News* all came in about 25 points left of the average. The *Washington Post, Morning Edition*, and *ABC World News Tonight* were less tilted, all about 15 points to the left.

Those shows and publications have all changed dramatically since then, as have the think tanks, so these scores don't do us any good in judging who is more fair today. But what it does tell us is that for a lengthy span in recent history, there was a pronounced leftward slant in almost all of the most important sources in the mainstream press. You can quibble with the methods and the scores for individual outlets, but this is as good an effort as I have seen to make the subjective estimation of media bias into some kind of objective measurement.

I'm sorry, conservatives, for what must seem like a belaboring of what to you is an obvious point. But I think this is such an important concept for understanding of the media industry, it's necessary to take some time on this for our liberal friends. Even if a person of the left is not willing to accept completely that there is substantial left-leaning or Democratic partisan bias in mainstream news, maybe they would at least allow why so many people think there is.

Gallup and the Knight Foundation, the heavyweight journalism nonprofit group, started collaborating in 2018 on the American Views project to measure public opinions about the news. Their 2020 report, titled "Trust, Media and Democracy," surveyed more than 20,000 American adults to ask about "how the news media delivers on its democratic mandate for factual, trustworthy information."[5] The answers were even more depressing than you might have feared:

- Sixty-five percent of Americans, including 57 percent of Democrats and 75 percent of Republicans, say the increasing number of news sources reporting from a particular point of view is "a major problem."
- A majority of Americans believed inaccurate news to be intentional—52 percent said because the reporter is misrepresenting the facts; 28 percent said they were making them up entirely.
- Seventy-four percent said news organizations they distrust are trying to persuade people to adopt a certain viewpoint.

Part of what's happening here is what I call the not-my-guy effect. It's what allows for Congress to consistently have national approval ratings somewhere below those for ringworm but an incumbency retention rate of more than 90 percent. "All the other guys are a bunch of four-flushing, no-account crooks, but not my guy," says Joe Madadatz or Suzy Creamcheese. "I met him at the charity softball game at the Elks Club a couple of years ago. He's not like the rest of them." So it is with the news: 64 percent said they were concerned about bias in the news that *other* people are getting, but only 34 percent were worried about their *own* news being biased. Even so, the fact that 65 percent of adults, including a stout majority of Democrats, think that biased news is a "major problem" for the country is unto itself alarming. And the fact that they see the bias as mostly intentional steers us away, rather than toward addressing the problem.

The belief that bias is the result of malign intentions is another example of fundamental attribution error at work. Intentional bias certainly happens, especially at outlets that profit by the click or minutes of viewership. We're also not talking about, say, those who dangle headlines about the unacceptable masculinity of female cartoon characters. Opinion journalism makes better clickbait explicitly because it is not trying to be fair. The question we're addressing is about bias in the news. And in the world of mainstream news, left-of-center outlets overwhelmingly predominate. There are several places on the conservative side that do scrupulous reporting and even some that mostly try to keep opinion out. But that leaves you with just a handful of sites like my own journalistic home, *The Dispatch*, maybe a few hours a day on Fox News and not much else.

Gallup-Knight's finding that 57 percent of adults see either "a great deal" or "a fair amount" of bias in the news source they rely on most often tells me that understanding goes well beyond GOP anti-press obsessives. I think they're right to be worried, but that the common perception that the slant is mostly intentional is wrong.

Many Republicans seem to think that reporters and editors see all of the points of view and then choose the ones that favor Democrats or liberal positions. I'm not saying that never happens, but the far more common problem in my experience is obliviousness. Republicans, people from Republican parts of the country, or even people who match the demographic characteristics of typical Republican voters are far less likely to go into journalism and media than other fields. The roots of the obvious left-wing bias in the news is more the product of *who* is doing that work than any intentional bias.

Our tendency is to see deficiencies as characterological rather than situational—back again to fundamental attribution error—so it may be hard to offer that benefit of the doubt to those who one believes have wronged her or his own tribe. But stick with me on this, conservatives. Big-time newsrooms tend to be liberal monocultures, and most journalists grew up in similar environments.

They're not cheating their audience so much as they are blind to the problem. If anything like 78 percent of political journalists are left-leaning, as the story selection study showed, Republicans are not participating in the news business at anything like the rates of their Democratic peers.

Gatekeeping is a factor here, no doubt. As in all kinds of work, the people who achieve success are likely to hire individuals who share their worldviews and backgrounds. That has always contributed to the leftward lean in hiring, going back to the widespread adoption of professional journalism in the middle of the previous century. But as newsrooms have worked hard to be more culturally inclusive and diverse, the tilt has almost necessarily been amplified.

If you are a woman who is part of an ethnic minority, grew up in the urban Northeast, went to Columbia Journalism School, and got your start with an alternative, progressive publication, human nature dictates that you will see job candidates with similar attributes as superior to others. It works that way for white dudes in finance from Connecticut who went to Wharton, and in every other field. Even if you're not making a conscious choice about the political leanings of a new reporter, your own implicit bias about a candidate's other characteristics will tend to set ideological boundaries. Female, minority, urban, Ivy League conservatives exist. But probably in about the same proportions of male, white, rural, SEC liberals.

The same innate biases that kept big-time journalism almost entirely the realm of white men for so long, work upon every new ruling class—just like all elites in all places in all times. Our own egos prove to be unconquerable. Indeed, efforts to defeat implicit bias in hiring when it comes to race and gender no doubt push newsrooms farther still to the left. If newsrooms were

already overwhelmingly white and liberal, setting hiring quotas
to emphasize individuals from groups that are left of the national
average would make it even harder to make room for reporters
whose backgrounds could help organizations battle against left-
wing groupthink.

But my guess is that gatekeeping is not the main driver of
the sharp tilt to the left among reporters, editors, and producers.
I think the biggest factors come down to political geography and
people following their hearts in a free society.

------

First, let's think about the red and blue map and where reporting jobs are and where they are going. It will surprise no one to
learn that as local newspapers have withered or died, it has inten-
sified a preexisting problem of geographical and cultural isolation for those who work in news.

According to the Bureau of Labor Statistics, 92 percent of
journalists worked in metropolitan areas in 2011, an increase of
nearly 20 points from fifty years before.[6] The Atlantic's Andrew
McGill estimated in the wake of the 2016 election that 13 percent
of all journalists worked within the less than twenty-three square
miles of the island of Manhattan.[7]

Here's Politico's Tucker Doherty and Jack Shafer writing
in 2017: "Today, 73 percent of all internet publishing jobs are
concentrated in either the Boston–New York–Washington–
Richmond corridor or the West Coast crescent that runs from
Seattle to San Diego and on to Phoenix.[8] The Chicagoland area,
a traditional media center, captures 5 percent of the jobs, with a
paltry 22 percent going to the rest of the country."

The result, they say: 72 percent of all internet publishing or newspaper employees in 2017 worked in a county won by Hillary Clinton. But Clinton only won about 16 percent of all counties.

I know that the population is far from evenly distributed. More than half of America's citizens live in fewer than 5 percent of counties, according to census data.[9] But that doesn't in any way minimize the social effects of having three-quarters or more of journalists working and mostly living in blue America.

Yes, people often move from red counties to blue counties for work, but the extreme urban concentration of the news media surely has a considerable effect. There is an obvious competitive advantage for aspiring journalists from urban, typically Democratic places since distance and relocation are factors as people consider their career paths. Then there is the power of social environment and the coalitional instinct. Peer and friend groups exert enormous power over individual perceptions, and if the universe of potential peers and friends where you live is only 20 percent or so Republican, there must be some effect in terms of self-censorship and groupthink.

A 2018 Pew study found that newsrooms were 8 points more male than the workforce in general: 61 percent, compared to 53 percent.[10] The same study found newsrooms were 12 points whiter than America's workforce as a whole, 77 percent to 65 percent. But some of the gaps shrank sharply among younger workers. The gender gap disappeared entirely among journalists under thirty, even as the whiteness rate remained consistent for all newsroom workers under fifty.

Let's compare those characteristics with a typically conservative or Republican sector, the energy industry, and then look more closely at a group of comparable size to the news industry:

those in the "fuels sector." That's the group that includes the major extractive industries like coal, natural gas, and oil. At the end of 2018, 1.1 million Americans were employed in the fuels sector, 79 percent of whom worked in oil or natural gas.[11]

That group was just 24 percent female, compared to 39 percent in newsrooms in the Pew study and a roughly even male/female split in the workforce overall. The degree of whiteness was about the same between journalism and fuels, landing in the mid-1970s, but think of the political implications of just the gender numbers alone. According to the AP VoteCast survey of 2020 voters, 58 percent of white men voted for Donald Trump. If the miners, riggers, drillers, and the rest of the fuels sector are almost twice as likely to be male as the national workforce, and about as white as the workforce as a whole, what might we guess about how that sector voted? Not a lot of Elizabeth Warren love over there, my friends.

Did they get into the business because they were conservative? Did they become Republican because of the perceived economic advantages for their industry? Does social pressure play a role? Do the places where there is mining, rigging, and drilling tend to be more red than blue? Do people in those industries tend to hire people like them? Yep, yep, yep, yep, yep.

I am so far the only coal salesman's son I have ever, to my knowledge, encountered working in national political journalism. People who grow up in places like Ohio County, West Virginia, and with families in the energy industry perhaps don't typically think about journalism jobs or find the work appealing. Indeed, given the terrible opinion we know Republicans have of the news media, there would be an obvious and strong disincentive for people from very Republican places from wanting to work in the news business.

You probably know intuitively or by experience that people in the news business are far to the left of people in coal, oil, and gas. That's no surprise. But I want you to think about the demographics of the newsroom when you try to understand how and why the media bubble got so thick. The energy industry leans Republican for many of the same reasons the news industry leans to the left: location and demographics.

I'm not suggesting geographic quotas for newsrooms in addition to the ethnic and gender diversity ones already in place. The hiring pool would shrink to nanoparticles if managers tried to impose both. But our friends on the left need to understand the truth of the saying "personnel is policy." Media personnel mostly come from and overwhelmingly work in blue America. Our friends on the right, meanwhile, need to acknowledge that the bias in journalism works the same way as the political leanings of other industries. The bias is implicit and born of groupthink far more than it is by design. Journalists are like coal miners when it comes to culture. They'd need a headlamp to see very far beyond the ends of their noses.

Left-leaning bias is real, but liberals and conservatives alike should please bear a couple of things in mind: 1) It is a result of cultural isolation and ignorance more than intent, and 2) there are other, in some ways more profound biases at work.

---

In the past few years, there has been a lot of anguishing over how the news media got the so-called Russiagate story so wrong, so often in so many different ways.

I don't here just mean how left-wing opinion mongers constantly overhyped the criminal investigations into former president Trump and his campaign's potential connections to the Kremlin, or how their right-wing counterparts worked themselves into a frenzy minimizing and deflecting allegations related to even the worst conduct by Trump & Company. If you were watching prime-time cable news or were reading Russo-obsessed sites day and night, one assumes you weren't looking for the straight dope on what was going on. You more likely wanted to be reassured that the story would turn out the way you wanted it to: Trump in manacles, frog-marched across the South Lawn, or Trump vindicated and his tormentors exposed and destroyed.

But we should care a lot less about that kind of fantasy role-playing than I do about the failures of the coverage that was intended to be credible and comprehensive. The appeal of clicks and ratings certainly played a considerable role in the failure of mainstream news organizations in getting the story right, in the same way it made Rachel Maddow and Sean Hannity or websites like the Palmer Report and American Greatness as preposterous as they were. But while ambition certainly played its role, a failure of this magnitude required more than just thirsty journalists or even the left-tilted bias that we discussed above.

On August 8, 2016, the *New York Times* took the unusual step of running the column of media writer Jim Rutenberg on its front page.[12] Under the headline "Trump Is Testing the Norms of Objectivity in Journalism" came some advice from the top media writer at the country's most influential newspaper to his fellow journalists. It was time for the impartial press to ditch the journalistic niceties and get in the fight against the Republican nominee:

> If you're a working journalist and you believe that Donald
> J. Trump is a demagogue playing to the nation's worst

racist and nationalistic tendencies, that he cozies up to anti-American dictators and that he would be dangerous with control of the United States nuclear codes, how the heck are you supposed to cover him?

Because if you believe all of those things, you have to throw out the textbook American journalism has been using for the better part of the past half-century, if not longer, and approach it in a way you've never approached anything in your career. If you view a Trump presidency as something that's potentially dangerous, then your reporting is going to reflect that. You would move closer than you've ever been to being oppositional. That's uncomfortable and uncharted territory for every mainstream, nonopinion journalist I've ever known, and by normal standards, untenable.

Rutenberg wrote that journalists had to move out of their comfort zones to stop Trump from exploiting notions of fair play and journalistic objectivity: "It may not always seem fair to Mr. Trump or his supporters. But journalism shouldn't measure itself against any one campaign's definition of fairness. It is journalism's job to be true to the readers and viewers, and true to the facts, in a way that will stand up to history's judgment. To do anything less would be untenable." Throw out the textbook, Rutenberg said, to keep Trump from getting the nuclear launch codes.

The piece caused a huge stir in newsrooms and was soon part of a larger, intense conversation about whether the rules of journalism were just weakening the power of the press to prevent a wicked man from becoming president. If Trump was a virus who was exploiting the media's own genetic structure to win, then they would have to change journalism's DNA. The debate about Trump and journalistic standards came after growing complaints about a lack of activist journalism and the dangers of "bothsidesism" that benefited the bad guys by false equivalence. With Rutenberg and the head of the *Times* politics team at the time, Carolyn Ryan, sounding the call, reporters were told that it was time to go to war with Trump.

Part of this was that many in the mainstream press felt guilty about having given Trump such a great platform from which to rain spitballs on his Republican rivals during the primaries. We'll explore that part in a later chapter in more detail, but you could see the thinking in real time: We brought Trump into this world, now we're going to take him out.

The problem was, though, that it didn't work. The mainstream press could not prevent Trump from becoming president. If anything, the explicit anti-Trump agenda played even more into the candidate's hands. When the front page of the "newspaper of record" says that it's trying to go after a candidate, it's pretty easy for that candidate to tell supporters the press is out to get him. The part where Rutenberg and Ryan explain that they're out to get Trump *because he deserves it* doesn't make it through the translation. Especially for Republicans raised on anti-media sentiment, a media jihad against the GOP nominee made it much easier to disregard the things about Trump that were genuinely concerning.

An old political joke I love goes, "Campaigns treat base voters like mushrooms: in the dark and covered with horse manure." All of Trump's Republican nominee predecessors had tried to explain for decades why voters should ignore unflattering stories in the "liberal media," but none of them ever had the press say it actually was on the grind. Just at the exact moment where it would have been most important for journalists to maintain the highest possible standards for objectivity, big-time news dove in the mud with Trump, where he had home field advantage. Their failure to stop him meant not only that a demagogue who, as Rutenberg said, exploits racist and nationalistic tendencies and cozies up to anti-American dictators was president, but also that the press was not as powerful as its elites had believed. The pain of Trump's victory wasn't just partisan bias in the press, it was personal and professional.

That doesn't mean that press coverage didn't play a powerful role in deciding the 2016 election, mind you. Whether or not outlets called Trump a "liar" or if he had been "untruthful" probably didn't make much difference, but the tidal motion of the news cycle sure did—and not in the way many in the media hoped.

Thirty days before the 2016 election, the *Access Hollywood* tape confirmed Trump was every bit the boorish, crude old fart in private as his public persona would have suggested. Trump bragged about grabbing women he had just met by the genitals and forcing them to kiss him.

A week later, Trump's campaign was close to death, Republicans were openly discussing whether he should step aside in a bid to save the Senate, and his poll numbers went in the toilet. It was the only time after the conventions that the GOP nominee fell below 40 percent in any high-quality national polls.[13]

But it was also the beginning of a remarkable comeback for Trump, who, now convinced that he was on his way to a Dukakis-sized defeat and lasting humiliation, got serious. Kinda. The following weekend he would travel to Gettysburg, Pennsylvania, where he would deliver a (mostly) telepromptered punch list of conservative priority points, including judicial appointments, tax cuts, and even term limits.

We all know the story. Trump buckled down—to the degree he could—just before then–FBI director James Comey and his crew jumped back in the race to announce the potential existence of more classified emails from the Democratic nominee. But this time the emails were on the icky laptop of sex offender Anthony Weiner, a former Clinton insider and then-husband of Hillary Clinton's top aide. Comey had butted in the election in July to announce that Clinton had been cleared of criminal wrongdoing in her mishandling of state secrets when she was secretary of state. Republicans seethed over Comey's intervention and he no doubt wanted to show his impartiality to GOPers who oversaw his agency and would still likely be in control of Congress after the election. But Clinton was a lock, so who on the Democratic side would care if Comey went a bit overboard in pushing the Weiner laptop story?

Sad trombone, Director Comey.

Trump's fear-driven discipline meant that the Weiner laptop dropped not into the usual burlesque of Trump's campaign and constant media outrage, but a more typical campaign climate. Trump had clawed back 4 points in the average of polls and, with a nudge from the FBI, that was enough to thread the needle in three big blue states to mark the most astonishing upset in modern political history. The combination of the *Access Holly-wood* tape, Comey's overconfidence, and the media's desire for something to cover meant that Clinton was leading the news at just the wrong moment. In 2016, both candidates were unpopular, so it was never helpful to either candidate to make persuadable voters dwell too much on them. And worst of all for Clinton, the late-breaking pseudo scandal (there was nothing new on the laptop) had reminders of so much that was unpleasant about the Clintons' would-be dynasty.

You can see how his compounding errors made Comey desperate to show that he was against Trump and to bring down or contain his presidency over Kremlin sympathies. Similar motives were present in the press. Not only had the decision to mud-wrestle with Trump shown the media to be far less powerful than its own elites imagined, but without Trump even trying, the press had followed a scandal cycle that very well could have made the difference in such a close race. The Russia story offered a way to make good on their failings in the campaign, and to apply the onesideism in a more studied, intentional way.

A word here about the actual facts of the case. America knew from the summer of 2017 that Trump's campaign had tried to collude with Kremlin sources to try to get dirt on Hillary Clinton—"very high level and sensitive information but is part of Russia and its government's support for Mr. Trump," as it was described in an email to Donald Trump Jr. from an associate looking for a meeting. The Trump team first lied about a meeting with Russian emissaries in Trump Tower that included Trump's campaign manager, son, and son-in-law. Then the line was that the meeting had been about facilitating U.S. adoptions of Russian children. Then the line was that yes, the meeting had taken place, but Trump himself found out about it along with the rest of the country. Then Trump admitted that he had written the press release lying about the nature of the meeting. It was an easy next step to the typically Trumpian response of saying that he had done it, he was glad he had done it, and that anyone else would have done the same thing.

As we would see even more clearly in 2020, Trump has few limits, if any, for what he would do to obtain and keep power. His ham-handed extortion of Ukraine's president for dirt on Joe Biden should have removed all doubt about Trump's disregard for decency in such matters. What Trump did before and after the November 2020 election to try to steal another term obliterated even that low standard. But even six months into Trump's term, everybody already knew that Trump's campaign had been thirsty for help from the Kremlin and was willing to lie about it.

But by then, the idea of something simple and obvious had been blown away by the Moby-Dick of Trump stories: the investigation led by Special Counsel Robert Mueller. Mueller, Comey's predecessor, had been tapped to lead the probe by the Justice Department after Trump fired Comey over, as the president would remarkably admit on the *NBC Nightly News*, the investigation into Russian election meddling. The Mueller probe offered a couple of important things to reporters, editors, and producers. First, a chance to finally bring Trump down, and second, month after month of exciting "big if true" stories that were impossible to disprove—an infinite well of intrigue.

And so began a two-year loop of anonymous tips, rank conjecture, and endless overhyping of irrelevant or decontextualized information nuggets. Outlets reported on Mueller's lunch habits, the subpoenas that may or may not have been sent, the lawyers who were seen going in and out of offices. Each passing week of obsessive coverage raised the expectations more and more for the findings. *Would Trump's children be indicted? Would Trump be indicted? Would Republicans turn on Trump like they finally did on Nixon with Watergate? Doesn't this really seem like Watergate, guys? Like really, really? Do you think the pee tape is real?*

When it was over, though, Mueller delivered a report that told us what we substantially knew: Russia tried to sow discord in the 2016 election and tried to help Trump get elected, including by hacking Democratic emails damaging to Clinton. Trump's campaign tried to collude with Kremlin emissaries at the Trump

Tower meeting, but some mix of incompetence and a desire for self-preservation by Trumpsters prevented the deal from being consummated. It was also later revealed that the FBI cut corners to get the wiretaps to surveil Team Trump. Moby-Dick swam out of sight.

So why were reporters so credulous about the rumors whirling through Washington? Part of it was obvious laziness and ambition, always a dangerous combination. Part of it was bias. Part of it was pride. Part of it was an overreliance on anonymous sources (a symptom of lazy ambition).

But how about elitism? That's part of the theory of populist media critic Matt Taibbi, as he lays it out in his book *Hate Inc.* and in his widely circulated newsletter. Taibbi, who rose to fame for his gonzo attacks on the financial industry and the Bush administration's foreign policy, has turned into a popular figure in some circles of the right for his attacks on cancel culture and the media in general. Like others in the left-right populist space, he sees economic elitism and moneyed interests as the cause of many problems in the press.

"The news business is absolutely different in a class sense than it once was, particularly at the national level," he writes in *Hate Inc.* "These days it's almost exclusively the preserve of graduates from expensive colleges, when it was once a job for working-class types who started as paper-kids or printers."

He says that journalists are now college-educated elites like the people they cover, and have lost the scrappy working-class spirit that once made them skeptical of the rich and powerful:

[T]he next generation of national political reporters viewed people in power as cultural soulmates because, at least socially, they were. While sportswriters for a while remained hardscrabble, cigar-chewing types who hammered team owners and managers for every tiny mistake, political reporters became professional apologists, constantly telling us how hard it is for politicians to win elections and run things.

Taibbi says that this class loyalty in journalists makes them too credulous about the claims of their fellow elites on things like Russiagate. Media critic Batya Ungar-Sargon makes a similar argument in her book, *Bad News: How Woke Media Is Undermining Democracy*. Increased college attendance among pressies, she says, led to a "status revolution" in the industry.[14]

In the 1930s, she writes, 30 percent of journalists had gone to college, by 1960 it was two-thirds, by 1983 it was 75 percent, by 1992 it was 82 percent, and by 2015, 92 percent had gone to college. Ungar-Sargon says one-third of Americans have a bachelor's degree and 46 percent have never attended a single college class, and that, she argues, helps set journalists apart as an elite caste.[15]

I'm certainly open to the idea that many in the news media are out of touch with the experiences and viewpoints of many of their fellow citizens. We spent quite a while in this chapter going over the geographical, cultural, and political isolation of many in the industry. But I'm not so sure about the idea of college being a major driver of those problems for the news business—or in profoundly different ways than other similar jobs. I certainly take Taibbi's point about the loss of a scrappy, irreverent sensibility that makes for good journalism. But if there is a college problem, it's hardly unique to the news business.

Ungar-Sargon cites research that says 30 percent of journalists had attended college in the 1930s, far higher than the 4 percent of the adult population in 1930 with bachelor's degrees or more, according to the data compiled by the National Center for Education Statistics.[16] In 1930, though, college was, like the newsrooms of the day, overwhelmingly white and male. We don't have numbers by race and gender prior to 1940, but even then, 6 percent of adult white males had college degrees compared to 1 percent of black men and 4 percent of white women. Black women with college degrees did not even register statistically.

It is surely true that the share of journalists with college degrees exploded between the 1930s and 1960, when Ungar-Sargon says college degrees in journalism doubled to include two-thirds of the workers in news. And it's also true, according to labor statistics, that only 8 percent of the adult population in 1960 had degrees. But guess who also doubled their college attainment levels since 1940? White dudes, who were still pretty much the whole story. If modern newsrooms, according to Pew, are three-quarters white and 61 percent male, just imagine what things looked like back in the Don Draper era.

In 1960, journalists were on track with the national trend for massive increases in college attendance driven by the GI Bill. The share would increase in rough symmetry to the national norms for adults and what we see in other white-collar jobs. By 2015, when 33 percent of all adults twenty-five and older were college graduates, Ungar-Sargon's research says 92 percent of news workers had gone to college. Industry-specific data on college degrees can be tricky by classification, but lots of other similar jobs saw massive increases in degree holders. Think of sales, agriculture, hospitality, or office management: jobs that may not require graduate degrees even for executive spots but where bachelor's degrees are now the norm for career-track workers. I doubt that was the case in the 1930s in those fields any more than it was journalism.

What about other vocations of similar socioeconomic status?

Schoolteachers are required to have degrees to meet accreditation requirements, but even there, you can see the college boom. In 1961, 15 percent of public school teachers had no college degree. By 1976, it was less than 1 percent, according to Department of Education reports. Even in their credentialed space, teachers are still nudging up a bit. In 2019, 4 or 5 percent of all public school teachers had doctorates, according to the Bureau of Labor Statistics.

Almost 77 percent of child, family, and school social workers have at least a bachelor's degree, nearly 40 percent of whom have advanced degrees, according to the Bureau of Labor Statistics.[17] Like with teachers, there are certification requirements that have driven those numbers up. But they are also a function of the same degree inflation that hit newsrooms and every other white-collar workplace. I doubt Taibbi and Ungar-Sargon would argue that having such a high percentage of college graduates among social workers has diminished their empathy for the people they're trying to help. Maybe the media critics would say that the membership of social workers in the caste of the college-educated has caused them to be less willing to fight existing power structures, as they allege of reporters. But I doubt it.

There are some jobs of similar status to reporters that don't have college-going rates that are as high. For instance, the Bureau of Labor Statistics classifies paralegals and legal assistants together and finds that this group includes 54 percent of workers without at least a bachelor's degree. But beyond that and a few other gigs, if you're working in what is now pretentiously referred to as the "knowledge sector," college is the norm, which means a degree just isn't the social stratifier it once was.

I am certainly willing to believe that the fetishization of college has had lots of bad consequences for American life, just not that it is unique to the news business. There's certainly something to the stifling effect of credentialing and academic elitism in big, national organizations. But I want to make sure that we're keeping the tens of thousands of newsroom workers and the thousands more who work in support roles in mind here, too. If you went to Columbia or another rarefied school with the same people you are covering, that's an implicit bias nightmare, to say nothing of the possibilities of outright back-scratching and favor trading. Ben Bradlee of the *Washington Post* was helping his fellow Harvard man John F. Kennedy hash out presidential speeches at night and then directing coverage as Washington bureau chief for *Newsweek* the next morning. That kind of thing no doubt still goes on today.

I'm not, however, worried about the fact that you need a college degree today to work in news, even if I wish more aspiring college journalists studied something *other* than journalism in school. We'll revisit that in the closing chapters, though.

But whatever college does or doesn't do to journalists, the bubble is real up and down the industry. The thickness may vary, but there is a barrier that is making matters worse. But what happened to create it? We know about how consolidation, isolation, implicit bias among bosses, and the free movement of labor and capital helped alienate the people from the press.

But there is something even more integral to consider.

———————————

There are lots of reasons that the vocation of journalism has evolved into a homogeneous tribe—a tribe that is badly out of touch with the needs and interests of the consumers it is supposed to be serving. But one of the causes is the standardization of the industry after World War II and the new professional, jargony language that standardization produced.

As we discussed in the previous chapter, there was lots of good that came out of the era, particularly the new emphasis on impartiality that national-scale broadcasting required. But this also invited a great deal of weasel wording. That's the newsroom term for "writing around" something difficult. If you don't want to offend anyone, you can hide your meaning in abstrusions and slink away, weasel-like.

C. S. Lewis was a stout champion of clear language, including in journalism. His 1943 book *The Abolition of Man* is a zealous denunciation of gushy, quavery language then growing in popularity among programmatic technocrats of the West. The slim volume is a thrilling harangue against the numbskull educators who are always looking for a way to define literacy, and thereby language, in pseudoscientific terms. Literacy isn't a phonetic understanding of words—the ability to read and write. It is your portion of the rich, dense cultural knowledge defined by our common language. Lewis was attacking what was—and very much still is—a systematic way to water down our words for the sake of a polite, bloodless way of talking that demands ample ambiguity. Corporate blabber, diversity blabber, legal blabber, technical blabber, and on and on and on.

"You can hardly open a periodical without coming across the statement that what our civilization needs is more 'drive,' or dynamism, or self-sacrifice, or 'creativity.' In a sort of ghastly simplicity we remove the organ and demand the function," he wrote in *The Abolition of Man*, which was first delivered as three evening lectures on "the teaching of English in the upper forms of schools" in 1943.

"We make men without chests and expect of them virtue and enterprise. We laugh at honour and are shocked to find traitors in our midst. We castrate and bid the geldings be fruitful."

Lewis saw that the way that children were being taught to speak, write, and think about language was directly at odds with the capacity for moral reasoning and its partner, clear understanding. Some areas of language have always been more prone to fluffy filigree; public life, business, and academia are chief among them. But Lewis saw ahead to where we live now, when the intentionally obfuscatory, feeling-based language of the politician or advertiser has become the everyday way we communicate with each other, and therefore how we think. Every emoji is a tiny squirt of squid's ink to obscure the bluntness of a message. Almost every business or government memorandum tries to build a big enough boulder of blather for the author to either hide under or roll on top of you.

The "chest," as Lewis described it, was the part of us that keeps an inventory of our passions, and, we hope, orders them virtuously. "The head rules the belly through the chest—the seat . . . of Magnanimity, of emotions organized by trained habit into stable sentiments."

Clear, strong, sincere words are necessary to put our attachments in the proper order and to maintain them. Whether you are a Christian like Lewis or not, there's no denying the need for virtuous order in the human heart. From classical philosophers to the Buddha to modern psychoanalysts, we have always known that some things are more important and more worthy than others. To sacrifice for the weak; to protect others; to tell the truth; to be free, to be just, to be merciful—all of these things fit the grooves of the human heart.

Mathematician and philosopher Blaise Pascal in 1670 said that within us was an "infinite abyss [that] can be filled only with an infinite and immutable object." A happy life, Lewis said, requires "the ordinate condition of the affections in which every object is accorded that kind of degree of love which is appropriate to it." Pascal and Lewis believed that infinite abyss could only be ordered by the God of the universe and His laws, but everyone knows the truth we teach to children: "If you don't stand for something, you'll fall for anything."

How we talk is how we think. How we think is how we order our affections. How we order our affections determines how we behave. How we behave determines how healthy we are as people and as a society. Without clear language, we can't describe virtue and vice, so we can't order our affections. One should choose carefully the opinions she or he is willing to stand up for—about who you are and what you believe—and let most of the rest of them go.

Or as they would say on the North Fork of Short Creek: "Opinions are luxury items; don't have more than you can afford." It matters whether you believe in the American system or the unalienable rights of all mankind. It doesn't matter whether you prefer hot fudge or butterscotch. (Butterscotch, obviously.) To decide what matters, we need healthy "chests," and those require clear language. But the clunky, self-validating kind of language that has anesthetized the American brain to such heroic-sounding considerations is everywhere.

The inanities of chestless language burst out like great geysers from the overflowing lake of bull that our society produces every day. Buying a house or checking into a hospital today uses loads more words than the founding documents of our civilization and some of the greatest works of philosophy. The Hertz car rental agreement, at 8,592 words, is almost twice as long as the Constitution. But these useless, boilerplate words of today are there to protect us from a very modern kind of disaster: being understood for saying what we mean.

We tell ourselves that we pile up language in this way so that we won't be misunderstood. Yes, a healthy discourse always requires some politesse, especially with strangers and with those who we love most. We should always choose our words carefully to be understood exactly as we mean and never in such a way that inflicts harm for its own sake. But often, what we really mean is that if you are deeply offended by what we say, we are only kidding. Or that if you think that we are wrong, we *did* acknowledge that the story or fact was "controversial" or that it was "reportedly" true. We can hedge and harrumph and look for a seam in the defense to bolt for a quick gain or escape to avoid a serious loss.

This is the tragedy of newsspeak, a kind of jargony, arch, verb-free chatter that pours into the infinite gullet for #content in the news business. It is wreathed in the superfluities of graduate school or boardroom gasbaggery that slow or destroy so much that is hopeful and good in the world. It is asphyxiating language used as protection but is truly deadly.

What Lewis warned Britain's educators about in his speeches would certainly apply to the unnecessary vamping and hippopotamus yawns that are passed off as debate or interview on a given day's TV news.

When words were more costly to journalists because of the restrictions of time and space, good news writing was about quick concision. The goal was to be as deeply understood as possible in the fewest words possible. But now we live in a news world that is less edited, more wordy, and that has less in common with the way people actually communicate. I find when writing a piece that won't appear in print, it's hard to resist the temptation to complicate what should be simple when I know that space is theoretically unlimited.

Of all the ways that the news business has weakened its relationship with consumers, the loss of a common language has to rank high on the list. And if we lose the ability to speak clearly, much trouble will come after.

# 4.

---

# WEAK PARTIES, STRONG PARTISANSHIP
## How the Siloed Media Hurts Democrats and Republicans

*My God, this is a hell of a job! I can take care of my enemies all right. But my friends, my God-damn friends, they're the ones that keep me walking the floor nights!*

—President Warren Harding, speaking to a reporter in June 1923[1]

My first meeting in Roger Ailes's boardroom of doom was on Election Day 2010. Republicans were poised to deliver a serious walloping to President Obama and roll back the Democrats' doughty majorities in both houses of Congress. The GOP was in position to score major wins in governors' mansions and statehouses from coast to coast.

The second floor of the NewsCorp headquarters on Sixth Avenue in New York was a hive of excited optimism. With Republicans looking forward to big wins, we knew viewership would be enormous that night. I was invited to the regular afternoon executive meeting for the first time so I could lay out the expectations we had on the Decision Desk and the politics team for what would transpire that night. I had only been with the company for about four months, and I was sweating it *hard* as I sat there at the far end from Ailes at a conference table roughly the size of a World War II aircraft carrier. The meeting was packed. Not only were executives from New York crowding in, but people like my boss Bill Sammon, who would have ordinarily joined the afternoon meeting by phone, were attending in person.

It felt like a steam bath in there, and I was running on about two hours of sleep and too many energy drinks. I had been up all night finishing the cards that we would use on the desk and the anchors would use on-air for quick reference guides on each race. They all had to be perfect (they still weren't), but I couldn't make my colleagues look foolish quoting my bad data. Plus, these were the five-inch by eight-inch little life rafts that I could hold on to as I tried to run the rapids of the many, many calls we were going to have to make that night. How many Republican votes in 2004 in Ozaukee County? When did the incumbent win his first term? What did the last polls say? Didn't her husband used to have that seat?

After four straight days and nights of data obsession and rehearsals, I had to now appear to be a normal human in front of a room full of New Yorkers to whom I assume I appeared to be a sweaty bumpkin. Yes, by the way, TV networks rehearse election nights with dummy numbers. The Decision Desk makes calls based on the pretend results to simulate the workflow and pinch points of the big night. If you're making one hundred calls, the hours between 9 p.m. and 11 p.m. are bound to be chaotic. Then the election night team uses the practice calls to test the graphics, lighting, anchor and guest positions, and communications. In six cycles working with that crew, we really learned how to make it hum. But in 2010, I was clueless.

So there I was, exhausted, tweaking on taurine and looking around the room at people who had been with the company
from the beginning. I was feeling very self-conscious. There was
even one guy who dyed the temples of his hair white like Paulie
Walnuts from *The Sopranos*. The smell of aftershave and coffee
was making me queasy. But I was the only one feeling that way.

The mood was jocular, and Ailes was having fun doing what
he liked best in the world: busting balls. The language of Fox
News in those days was definitely locker-room swagger. Men
and women alike tried to match Ailes's tough-guy energy. His
top lieutenant, Bill Shine, carried it off perfectly. He grew up
on Long Island, the son of a police officer. Shine didn't talk too
much, but he made the words count. And like Ailes, he never
missed a chance to crack on someone, usually in an avuncular
way. Razzing people over their teams, their neighborhoods, or
whatever was at hand was the language of belonging on Ailes's
crew. Bill O'Reilly, for all his clashes with management, was the
avatar for these folks: suburban New York, Roman Catholic,
traditional values but not necessarily social conservatives—the
*New York Post*, not the *New York Times*.

I was definitely out of place. I had never been to New York as
an adult until I started going up for Fox. I knew about as much
about the TV business as a horse knows about making a saddle.
It's possible I was wearing a bow tie. As the execs went around
the table offering the boss their updates, I rehearsed my lines in
my head. Sammon teed me up, and I started racing through time
zones and expected times for calls and generic ballot trends until
Ailes interrupted to say, "What's your number?" The number, of
course, was how many seats I forecast Republicans to win that
night. "Our best guess is sixty-four seats, sir." Ailes, mouth set
like a bulldog and eyes staring through the back of my head,

said, "Dick Morris says it could be one hundred. Why is yours so low?"

I figured Ailes, a smart man, knew that Morris was a joke. Morris had not yet reached the comic heights in his pronouncements that he would in 2012 and beyond, but the former Clinton advisor turned Republican Pollyanna was already pretty clearly making stuff up. In 1874, after Republicans lost the whole South at the end of Reconstruction and during a financial panic and with a scandal-plagued GOP administration in the White House, they lost ninety-six seats.[2] Obamacare was unpopular and all, but there just weren't enough competitive seats on the post-1994 map to make such a number possible.

Morris said goofy stuff like that, I assumed, because it got him on TV. Sean Hannity in particular would bring Morris on to say that the red wave was a Krakatoa-sized tsunami that would change politics forever. They, and some other analysts who I previously thought were more principled and smarter than Morris, used the same routine for the 2012 presidential election. That time they made preposterous claims not only that Mitt Romney was obviously going to win, but that it would be by a landslide. The best I could say for Romney in that cycle was that he had a path to a narrow victory by picking off a couple of Blue Wall states if he could turn things around in Ohio, where he had been sucking wind all summer. But a landslide? Pish posh.

That one-hundred-seat number in 2010 was just hype to juice ratings, and Ailes had to know that. Right? He was messing with the new guy. Right?

But I wasn't sure. I didn't say what I thought: Morris is feasting on the carcass of journalism like a lamprey eel on a dead nurse shark. But maybe Ailes believed the hype. I instead carefully explained how I had worked with the all-stars in our then-great

Brainroom to check every seat and every estimate to make sure we were on the money. Ailes left me with "You'd better hope you're right . . ." and I walked out in the herd of suits in a haze. I had just disputed the maximum leader of Fox News and talked down Republican chances in a room full of people flying high on the thought of a ratings bonanza. I would eventually learn to say what I was thinking, lampreys and all. It served you better with Ailes, who in those days appreciated honest disagreement on his team. It was partly his scorpions-in-a-bottle management style, but also that he genuinely seemed to think it was better to air out disagreements. Bust balls or be busted.

I sat on those House races like a mother hen all night until we were able to make the call for the sixty-fourth net pickup for Republicans sometime in the wee small hours. We hit the number right on the screws, and I had delivered on my accidental called shot in the boardroom. I rode adrenaline through a day and a night of on-air hits and then slept the whole way home on the train.

The lesson I learned was that Hannity, Morris, and the rest of the crew of the crimson tide were certainly engaging in wishful thinking, but certainly also motivated reasoning. The story they were telling was good for ratings or the frequency of their appearances. They wanted it to be true because they wanted Republicans to win, but keeping viewers keyed up about the epochal victory close at hand was an appealing incentive to exaggerate the GOP chances. It was good for them to raise expectations, but it wasn't good for the party they were rooting for.

Early in an election cycle, crafty partisans want to play up their side's chances. It helps their candidate recruitment and fundraising and may lead vulnerable incumbents on the other side to just go ahead and retire. But at the end of a cycle, the preferred message whenever possible should be that the race is tight-tight-tight—every vote could be the winning vote, so don't forget to cast your ballot. Ask Hillary Clinton how overconfidence can depress turnout as marginal voters opt to stay home. It occurred to me in 2010 and was confirmed to me in 2012 that despite all that Fox's detractors said about the network being a mouthpiece for the Republican Party, the two organizations had fundamentally different aims.

Good politics is often bad TV. As much as we rightly lament the decline of the American electorate's aspirations and expectations, at least a plurality of voters still clearly prefer competency, cooperation, and decency. And what could be more boring than that?

I don't mean that it isn't helpful for politicians and their teams to be gifted at doing television and understanding its power. Donald Trump was a better producer than some professionals I have seen. I once watched him on a feed telling a crew how to set the lights for an interview like he had worked as a director for decades. He may have run his presidency like a reality show, but no one could say the man did not understand the medium of television.

Indeed, Trump's decades on television playing a playboy businessman and ultimately hosting a game show for other celebrities for fourteen seasons on NBC was what really made him president. He was a product of television more than any American president before and, probably, ever again. Ronald Reagan and Bill Clinton were both good *on* television. Trump *was* television.

In February 2019, Trump invited to the White House the parents of a British teenager killed in a traffic accident with the wife of an American diplomat. The woman had fled Britain, claiming diplomatic immunity, but was wanted by authorities in

the United Kingdom for the charge of causing death by dangerous driving. Her flight from prosecution was turning into a real
international incident, and the teen's parents were not easily
mollified. So after a fifteen-minute meeting in the Oval Office,
Trump sprang the big reveal on them: The woman wanted in
conjunction with their son's death was in the next room.[3] Did
they want to meet her? Shocked, they refused, saying the only
place they wanted to meet her was on British soil after she had
faced charges. It was a blunder politically, but it would have been
*great* TV. All that was missing was Oprah Winfrey to conduct
the tearful post-meeting interview.

As we will see in the next chapter, outlets left and right
initially loved Trump because while he was bad at politics, he
knew how to make compelling television. Trump was able to
use the power of TV to get around the fact that he very often
did not know what he was doing or talking about. He knew the
poses and how to either keep the narrative arc going or change
story lines. If he was in trouble, you could rely on Trump to keep
throwing out plot twists. He'd toss out some crazy-sounding line
or diabolical insult on Twitter in one of his many gaggles with
reporters, hoping that the press would chase the pointless but
more sensational-sounding issue. Guess what? We usually did.

Here were some of the hits from his unhappy 2018 midterm
year: "Trump floats pay bonus for teachers who carry guns in
class;"[4] "Trump proposes state-run tv network;"[5] "Trump floats
season suspension for NFL players protesting anthem;"[6] "Trump
blasts 'treasonous' Democrats for not applauding at his State of
the Union address."[7] Each of these inanities led to serious coverage, outrage, and sometimes even fact checks. The *Washington
Post* launched a whole podcast to track Trump's weapons-grade
malarkey called *Can He Do That?* Most of the time, the answer

was that Trump wouldn't even remember the rabbit he let loose by the next day. Alas, reporters had so burned out news consumers on truth-squadding Trump's loony logorrhea that the more serious wrongdoing in which he engaged got lost in the flow.

However, I understand why fact-checking Trump was sometimes irresistible. My all-time favorite Trump fabrication came from the time he tried to hold the G7 economic summit at his Doral golf resort in Florida but couldn't get around all of the obvious ethical problems. When asked about it, Trump said it was not about his business, but logistics: "Best location. Right next to the airport, Miami International—one of the biggest airports in the world. Some people say it's the biggest."[8] As if this were an unknowable, subjective thing that people debated, like asking who were the best first basemen of all time. (They are Lou Gehrig, Stan Musial, and Albert Pujols, if you're wondering.) Trump had no idea what he was talking about. Miami International Airport was 38th largest in the world and 11th largest in the United States by volume of passenger traffic.[9] Having a person make stuff up so often would be enough to drive any reporter into fact-check overdrive.

The correct thing for Trump to do in the political interests of his party in 2018 would have been to have a disciplined message focusing on economic growth and some other strong points for his administration. Unpopular, first-term presidents should keep a low profile in a midterm year to give vulnerable incumbents some breathing room. That would have been good politics for Republicans, but terribly boring television. Whether it was his supporters in the media or his many critics, they wanted more Trump, and the wilder the better. And he agreed.

The divergent interests between the news media and the parties would be a good thing if the institutions were fulfilling their appointed duties. But what happens when the work of parties gets outsourced to news outlets?

———————————

I opened my mailbox recently to find a very alarming mailer, printed in bright red ink. It looked like political junk mail, but it was actually from the once eruditely liberal *New Republic*. It went like this:

### STOP THE RIGHT-WING CRAZIES
Their attacks on our democracy have got to end
(And they're about to get a whole lot worse.)

Inside, the magazine's editor, Michael Tomasky says, "Let's be clear from the start. America is at war. We're locked in an existential confrontation between democracy and authoritarianism." He goes on at length about how "democracy is hanging in the balance" and other super-scary scenarios. And what should we do about these threats to our existence? Why, send $16.97 for a subscription, silly!

Tomasky is going to stop exactly zero "right-wing crazies," because basically nobody to the right of Elizabeth Warren ever sees the magazine. If you're reading the *New Republic*, your vote probably isn't any more up for grabs than a reader of Breitbart News. If you're enough of a junky to subscribe, you're certainly a likely voter and, in general elections where you would oppose said crazies, your vote is already in the bank.

And if America really is "at war" in "an existential confrontation," I doubt what you're going to want to be packin' is a story about Ikea's lust for Romanian hardwoods and the company's environmental hypocrisy.[10]

So why is a magazine that once prided itself on its detached eggheadery selling itself like a Steve Bannon scam PAC? It's partly the same reason that the American Civil Liberties Union is morphing from being an obstreperous defender of free speech and individual rights to being just another clickbaity, small-dollar-donation hustling, left-wing group, including running campaign ads. Why do venerable institutions, as one former ACLU director said, risk "surrendering [their] original and unique mission in pursuit of progressive glory"?[11]

Part of it is money. Scam PACs are so common because they work, at least for their proprietors. Apocalyptic language, panic-inducing pleas, and exploiting the latest culture war controversy may seem so blatant that anyone can see through it, but as political operatives have told me for years, none of that matters when it's just you and your phone there in the dark. You may have never made a rage donation, but have you ever bought something preposterous while scrolling online? Did you ever have a third glass of wine, go on social media, and then a week later find a *Saved by the Bell* lunchbox, miracle tape that you can make into a bass boat, or a fifteen-dollar bottle of hot sauce in a mailing pouch on your front porch?

Small-dollar campaign-style donations have been such a bonanza for ostensibly nonpartisan organizations because of the same principle that makes online impulse buying so dangerous. The individual amounts seem small, so who cares if it looks a little scammy? If you're already wound up about an issue, and you get the solicitation at just the right moment, you may click. What's five dollars if we're trying to end racism? What's $16.97 for a subscription if "America is at war" and we need more articles decrying Larry David's support for cryptocurrency to save democracy?[12] The click and the digital donation soothes the giver. It makes them feel virtuous and, for a time, eases their guilt about not doing their part.

But there's something else: These institutions are filling a vacuum left by America's failing political institutions.

You've probably heard the infamous line from Representative Matt Gaetz, the shock-jock congressman from the northern part of Florida's Gulf Coast: "If you aren't making news, you aren't governing." He made the comment, aptly, to *Vanity Fair* in an interview that would make even the most cynical observer of American politics despair. The truth, of course, is the opposite of Gaetz's motto: When you are making news, you're not governing.[13]

If you're in Congress, the "news" part is mostly supposed to come before and after the "governing" part. You might have some moments when you have to negotiate in public a bit—"While I admire Senator Claghorn's willingness to keep the conversation going, we remain committed to a bill that . . ."—but in a healthy system, the coverage is supposed to be a reward for achievement. Picture the victors, hands clasped, held high at the signing ceremony, or the golden shovels at the groundbreaking. But that means impulse control and delayed gratification. For the very online, mostly younger members of both parties in Congress, that's just not going to do it. If Representative Alexandria Ocasio-Cortez really wanted to raise taxes on the wealthy, she wouldn't do it by writing "tax the rich" on her rump and going to the Met Gala. But if she wants to be *famous* for wanting to raise taxes on the wealthy, then she's right on track.

But it was another part of the same *Vanity Fair* story about Gaetz that gave us his koan of political narcissism that really caught me. It was an excerpt from his book, *Firebrand*, which I had successfully managed to avoid:

"Politics, they say, is show business for ugly people. The real question is who writes the scripts and produces the acts. You are governed by the theater geeks from high school, who went on to make it big booking guests on the talk shows," Gaetz writes. "Ignore them and they'll ignore you, and you'll go nowhere fast. The hairdressers and makeup ladies and cameramen pick our presidents. As well they should. They are closer to the viewers and therefore the voters."

Now remember, this is written by a guy whose job title is *representative*. I love my friends who work in TV news, but why would we think a makeup artist in Washington, DC, or New York is closer to the voters than a congressman from the Flora-Bama coast who was raised there and represented portions of it for a dozen years, starting as a state representative? He is provided by taxpayers with ample funds to return home often and should have a better grasp of what regular folks are thinking than almost anyone. But to Gaetz, the men and women of TV land have special powers and perceptions and can use them to save or damn suppliants like the congressman.

But "the theater geeks from high school" who Gaetz says "went on to make it big booking guests" don't think they've "made it big." They're underpaid, overworked, and spend their time mostly getting turned down for interviews by people with real power and then having to deal with thirsty backbenchers like Gaetz to try to grind out another forty-four minutes of news-like content to put around ads for copper skillets and prelubricated pocket catheters.

As much as I would personally prefer the benevolent rule of the TV bookers I know to the current political class, we are not "governed" by them. While Gaetz is certainly an extreme example of the inversion of Congress, his misunderstanding about what power and governance are is instructive about the problems with the institution as a whole. Media coverage is supposed to be a means to an end, not an end unto itself. The reverential tones with which Gaetz talks about television suggest that he and the other members who engage in what Yuval Levin describes as "performative outrage for a partisan audience" don't want power nearly as much as they want celebrity.

"They remain intensely ambitious, as politicians always are, but their ambition is for a prominent role in the cultural theater of our national politics, and they view the institution of Congress as a particularly prominent stage in that theater," Levin writes in his book *A Time to Build.*[14]

Levin, in addition to being my boss at the American Enterprise Institute, is probably the foremost conservative champion of restoring Congress to its rightful place atop the constitutional order. But that can't happen if the members of the institution itself see their positions primarily as "a way to raise their profiles, to become stars in the world of cable news or talk radio, to build bigger social media followings, and to establish themselves as celebrities."[15]

If members of Congress believe that former drama nerds and camera operators are governing the country, then who the hell actually is?

———————————

Our Founding Fathers had a moral imagination and an understanding of human nature possessed by only a few people throughout time. Like Augustine of Hippo or William Shakespeare, the Founders saw mankind more clearly than their peers, both in their own age and across history.

But there is only one thing that I'm aware of that escaped even the combined moral genius of Alexander Hamilton, James Madison, Thomas Jefferson, John Jay, and George Washington: that one branch of government would intentionally give up its own power.

They were certainly worried about the new Congress being subject to bribery, foreign and domestic, and of the dangers of self-dealing. And Jefferson and the Anti-Federalists were hypervigilant about the dangers of a presidency of expansive powers. If you could show them the way the presidents of this century have openly flouted the constitutional limits on their power, the Founders might be saddened, but probably not surprised. They were very familiar with executive abuses from George III. But what I believe would truly surprise the Founders is what a pitiful creature Congress has become. Members are lickspittles to presidents of their own party and basically disengaged when the White House is in opposing hands, waiting for their turn to be toadies again.

The problem isn't that presidents are greedy for power. The problem is that Congress isn't.

The innate human desire for control is the engine that drives every government, including here in the land of the free. But the premise for preventing the abuse of power, as Madison put it perfectly in *Federalist* No. 51, is that "ambition must be made to counteract ambition." The cure for an imperial presidency is a legislative branch that fights the executive not just on policies, but for power itself. The members of the House and Senate should understand that their role is to maintain the boundaries of divided government so they can have more of what they want now, but also as custodians for future Congresses. And it wasn't just in the era of powdered wigs and waistcoats that leaders understood that.

The cousins Roosevelt stand among the most imperious of all American presidents. So it is no surprise that they held our judiciary—the most republican of our branches—in low esteem. Both were populists who despised the fogeyism of judges who would not bend to the will of popular sentiment or take a permissive view of what "emergency" might allow the Constitution to be shelved.

After leaving office in 1909, Teddy Roosevelt raged at his handpicked successor, William Howard Taft. Taft, along with the conservatives in Congress and the courts, rejected Roosevelt's vision of a larger, more powerful federal government.[16] Roosevelt broke his promise to not seek a third term and campaigned in 1912 against Taft for the Republican nomination. After he lost, he started his own Progressive Party, split the Republican vote, and guaranteed that Woodrow Wilson and the Democrats would win in November.

One of Roosevelt's key proposals was for a system in which judicial rulings could be overturned by plebiscite.[17] After hearings and appeals, a Supreme Court ruling would be put to the voters the next year. Roosevelt wanted to be able to intimidate the Court into giving him what he wanted. I get bilious just imagining how terrible those culture war contests would be under such a scheme today.

We can certainly imagine today how a bitter split within a party's presidential candidates—including a wealthy, mercurial, power-hungry former president from New York—could arise. Taft's decision to stand up to Roosevelt and the populists in 1912, even if it meant certain defeat in the general election, was not what we've mostly seen from the conservatives of our day, but we can see it faintly sketched in their intentions.

But how about a Congress of a president's own party, including his vice president, defying a commander in chief who had just won a landslide reelection, carrying all but two states and 61 percent of the popular vote?

Franklin Roosevelt had managed in his first term to get a lot of leeway from the courts on emergency measures to deal with the Great Depression. But when it came to his desires to create permanent changes to the nature of American government, the courts said no. After he won reelection in 1936, Roosevelt sought his revenge.[18] Claiming that the justices of the Supreme Court were too old to handle the very busy modern caseload—the court rejected 87 percent of cases, after all—he wanted to give them a hand, or twelve. Roosevelt sought the power to appoint an additional justice, up to a total of six more, for each sitting member over age seventy years and six months.

It was a scandal. After four years of conservatives warning that Roosevelt was a despot, he came charging into his second term seemingly trying to prove them right. He instructed the Democratic supermajorities in both houses of Congress to expand the Court from the nine justices it had comprised since 1869. With the new seats he could pack the Court with his picks, who would share his capacious ideas of presidential authority.

But it wasn't the small, noisy conservative minority that sank FDR's power play. It was moderate Democrats in Congress. Roosevelt's vice president, former House Speaker John Nance Garner of Texas, had been instrumental in winning passage of key New Deal provisions. Working with his acolyte and successor in the House, Sam Rayburn, and using his post as president of the Senate to lobby the upper chamber, Garner was a key to FDR's first-term success.

As Roosevelt's ambitions grew and grew, Garner became uneasy—but it was the court-packing that tore it.[19] Garner, who jealously guarded the power of Congress, knew what he saw coming: a president with a puppet court to affirm his actions steamrolling the legislative branch for years to come. With the help of Judiciary Committee chairman Henry Ashurst of Arizona, Garner and the institutionalists bottled up the bill—much to the frustration of Roosevelt and his Senate enforcer, Majority Leader Joe T. Robinson of Arkansas.

It was the end of any partnership between Roosevelt and Garner—who would later describe the vice presidency as not being worth "a pitcher of warm piss."[20] By 1940, when Roosevelt was poised to throw over Washington's two-term standard, Garner was jockeying to block him at the Democratic convention and Roosevelt had replaced him on the ticket with a true radical on executive power, then–agriculture secretary and Soviet enthusiast Henry Wallace.[21]

Roosevelt did end up getting to "pack" the Court in his own way. By flouting the Washington standard and running four times, FDR got to entirely remake the Supreme Court, making nine appointments in all. But thanks to Garner and the defenders of Congress, some leash was left to try to constrain the executive branch. When Mitch McConnell refused Donald Trump's demand to drop the Senate's sixty-vote threshold for legislation or when Joe Manchin did the same to Joe Biden, they were relying in part on power that Garner helped preserve.

But the number of lawmakers like McConnell and Manchin willing to refuse even weak presidents of their own party when it counts is pretty small these days. So where did all the "Cactus Jack" Garners go? They've been replaced by the Machiavellis of the makeup room like Gaetz and Ocasio-Cortez.

Congress has been devolving its own power for decades, outsourcing its constitutional duties to the executive and judicial branches. While they let agency bureaucrats and unelected judges legislate, lawmakers busy themselves with raising money and generating clicky sound bites in the hopes of attaining the nirvana of permanent incumbency and eternal celebrity. Unfortunately for us, that means avoiding hard choices whenever possible. And what is governing but making hard choices?

Perhaps what the Founders couldn't foretell was that one day, thanks to cable news and the internet, there would be an almost unlimited amount of attention available to even unimpressive legislators. I am glad that George Washington et al. did not foresee our current celebrity-obsessed culture, because they may have decided to scrap the whole deal if they had seen one episode of *Keeping Up with the Kardashians*. Celebrity didn't really arrive in Western culture until one hundred years ago with the motion picture and Charlie Chaplin. It works strange magic on the human mind and spirit.

People have always been willing to trade power for money, hence the Founders' concerns about improper emoluments and the bestowal of foreign titles. Now people will trade power just to be famous—and not even actually famous, but Twitter and cable news famous! To achieve political fame in a world where news was inherently limited in space and time, a leader had to be very successful. When there were only so many columns of newsprint and minutes of a television or radio broadcast, it took some doing to become a household word. Senators Huey Long, Joe McCarthy, and many others proved that you didn't have to be successful in your legislative efforts to be famous, but they did have to work awfully hard for the airtime. Now totally undistinguished lawmakers with no clout at all can connect to a social media river of intense, if artificial, connection with fervent fans.

If these aspiring celebrity lawmakers want to get really famous, though, they still need the news. And if the goal is to get on TV, then they had better not be boring. They had better deliver the "performative outrage for a partisan audience" that Levin described because, as we've seen again and again, that is the business model for news in a fragmented marketplace. Acting that way, though, basically precludes one being an effective lawmaker. Members like Jim Jordan, a Republican from Ohio, or Ocasio-Cortez can use the celebrity approach to secure power inside their own conferences, but can't advance much legislation. Doing so would require cooperation with moderate members of one's own party and even some members of the other party.

That would mean showing good faith, avoiding ad hominem attacks and other cheap shots. It would also mean actually avoiding news coverage for significant periods of time in order to work out details on proposals before going public. Heaven forfend . . .

The incentives that partisan leaders have to offer for good conduct and constructive participation are as out of date as Jack Garner's high collar. Working up through committee slots to get plum posts that can be used to steer pork or other favorable legislation to the voters back home still works for some. But what many members want in the way of committee postings are the ones that reliably produce high-visibility hearings. But, of course, once leaders give them the prime slots, they will use them for grandstanding and performative anger, which further undermines congressional authority. Congressional oversight hearings are increasingly just cheesy daytime soap operas with less appealing cast members.

The partisan news model requires reliable servings of red meat that will not alienate core segments of the audience, even as it renders effective legislation impossible. That increases voter frustration because Congress can't do its job, which generates a larger audience for performative outrage. As it stands at this writing, there are enough members in both parties in a narrowly divided Congress who really think the booking producers are governing the country, that it makes even ordinary work like budgeting extremely difficult. Every must-pass bill creates a new opportunity for celebrity lawmakers to go sprinting for the camera positions in the Russell or Cannon office buildings to start making unrelated demands and promising hell to pay.

Rational parties with the power to enforce even modest order would insist on boring competence in ordinary matters, since that's what persuadable voters would rather see. But they can't compete with the lure of the red light on the camera that tells ambitious members that it's showtime.

---

Of all the kinds of work I have done in journalism, presidential debates have been among the most fun and satisfying. In the 2012 and 2016 cycles, I got to help put together multiple debates for Fox News. They were all on the Republican side, but not for lack of trying. So much cajoling, pleading, and meeting with Democratic candidates and party officials in both cycles led to naught.

I understand why it would have been against the perceived self-interest of the Democratic candidates to participate. The way debates worked prior to the 2020 cycle was that networks and their partners—a newspaper, a college, etc.—would run the events on their own. That meant obtaining commitments from the front-runners, knowing that the rest of the candidates would show up for the chance to take shots at the leaders of the pack. Or it could go the other way: Get enough other candidates to participate so that the front-runners, who usually perceive debates as undesirable risks, have to participate or else look like chickens. In 2012, the last presidential election of the old regime, Republican front-runner Mitt Romney shunned the debate stage for months as other candidates jumped into the spotlight. While Romney was raising money, candidates like Herman Cain, Rick Santorum, and Newt Gingrich were chomping the scenery in debates. Nine, nine, nine, y'all.

Our debate team was, in my obviously biased opinion, the best in the business. But even Fox's toughest critics on the left would have allowed that Bret Baier, Megyn Kelly, and Chris Wallace were tough, fair moderators. We spent weeks researching, refining, and gaming out the questions under Bill Sammon's leadership. Each question had to be factually accurate, germane, and aimed at helping primary voters make a better decision about their choice. The goal was always to avoid cheap-shot "gotcha" questions.

But by 2020, the old conventions had already broken down. Rather than debates hosted by journalists, Democrats were looking for safer spaces for their candidates. The Democratic National Committee stepped in to arrange debates itself. In 2016, Republicans had decided to punish candidates who participated in debates unsanctioned by the party. But in the next cycle, Democrats took the next step of becoming television producers.

This was bad news for the press, but also for the party. Yes, they got opinion hosts like Rachel Maddow and Don Lemon as questioners instead of just news anchors and reporters. That's fun for the party faithful at home, but misses the point of debates.

Instead of questions that will reveal candidates' qualities in a general election contest as well as their positions on the issues that matter to party members, they get either softballs about how rotten the other side is or niche questions that invite pandering to base voters. In debate after debate in 2020, the questioners tilted the stage toward Bernie Sanders and Elizabeth Warren in part because that's what the hosts' fans would have wanted. That pushed the whole field toward answers that would be liabilities in the fall.

But there's more at work here, too. While Republicans certainly are the most effulgent in their hatred of the press, the Democratic base has its media demons, chief among them Fox News. I can make a strong case that Democrats would have been better off to face the Fox debate team in 2016 and 2020 and would have gotten scrupulously fair treatment. But I also know why that was a political impossibility. If we had somehow convinced the DNC to go along in 2020 or gotten the major candidates to participate in 2016, base voters would have been furious at party leaders. And any candidates who did agree to participate would have been vulnerable to accusations of aiding the enemy.

We've all seen presidential primary debates where the moderators are acting either as issue advocates or, the equally undesirable alternative, questioning from a general election perspective. With the latter, it usually goes nowhere, and sometimes even makes a juicy pitch for a candidate to smash by complaining about the media. The right question isn't "you're a meanie, defend yourself." It is: "If you win, your general election opponent is going to call you a meanie because of the things you have said and done. Why should these voters take on that baggage for their party?" I understand that may sound like semantics, but it's crucial framing. The primary debate moderator and the general election debate moderator come in the stead of two different sets of voters. As Wallace showed in his performances in both primary and general election presidential debates, they are not the same arts—even if they are ones at which he is equally adept.

If a primary debate question to a Republican asks, "Why aren't you taking a harder stance on climate change?" or to a Democrat asks, "Couldn't your proposed tax increases slow the economy?" it may sound adversarial, but it is not in any way revealing. First, persuadable general election voters are not likely to be watching. If you're tuning into a prime-time presidential debate, chances are that you are a political junkie. And if you're a political junkie, there's little chance that you're a persuadable voter. There's a strong correlation between political engagement and partisanship. So there's little worry for debate participants about offending the audience at home with red meat for the primary electorate. Second, it makes the questioner an easy foil for the candidates.

Donald Trump was hardly the first candidate to see the utility in clobbering questioners, nor is it limited to the GOP. Bernie Sanders loved to go full Festivus on questions from the "corporate media." But even these kinds of fake-tough questions are probably going to be too much for the parties and the networks going forward—and news networks will likely agree. I watched Fox News viewers rage at Kelly, Wallace, and Baier for asking tough, fair questions to candidates across two cycles. In 2016, Trump and his supporters particularly went bananas over obvious questions about his bankruptcies, refusal to back the party's eventual nominee if he lost, and, famously, degrading comments about women. Tellingly, network executives offered only a nominal defense and continued to offer Trump friendly interviews from which he could continue his attacks on the news division. This was the first of many further depredations to come.

Parties need real primary debates to help weed out bad candidates because there are so few settings in which office seekers will face any kind of accountability.

Whatever the office, candidates know that there's little reason to submit oneself to tough questioning. That's nothing new. The love affair between *60 Minutes* and candidate Barack Obama was so intense in 2008 that it eventually resulted in CBS offering a DVD for sale of the tenderest moments between Obama and interviewer Steve Kroft. Relive every giggle and meaningful pause! Obama felt obliged in the general election to occasionally submit to some tough, sit-down interviews. But as a primary candidate, who but a fool would want to face rigorous questioning, even if it was fair? And, with communications advisors telling them to expect unfairness, who needs it at all?

Indeed, a candidate's goal is usually to surf through the primary season with minimal contact with nonpartisan media. The only reason not to is to try to get attention for a struggling campaign by dumping on his or her own party. You can generally tell how well a primary candidate is faring just by the media outlets he or she is choosing. Long after Fox News lost interest in booking former front-runners in past cycles, MSNBC and CNN would still happily give them airtime to dump on the GOP front-runner. It works in reverse, too. Sanders's willingness to do Fox specials in 2016 and 2020 was closely correlated to the size of his deficit to Hillary Clinton and Joe Biden.

The problem for the country and the parties, then, is that candidates can too often get through what is supposed to be a vetting process without ever going to see the horse doctor.

A reminder here about our previous discussion of America's disastrous primary system. Our general election politics are not pretty, but the basic idea of encouraging candidates to seek consensus still seems intact. In 2020, for example, Donald Trump almost never mentioned immigration and paid for Spanish-language advertisements because he could not afford to alienate any potential Hispanic support in Florida, Texas, Arizona, and Georgia. Joe Biden scoffed at "defund the police" and ran on explicit bipartisanship because he could not afford to alienate any potential support from moderate suburbanites. These things are contrary to what Trump and Biden said and did as primary candidates, but this is an understood convention of American politics.

The news media manages to accommodate this all quite well. In an evenly divided country, quadrennial presidential elections are good for business. A close race generates not just extra advertising revenues, but more intense consumption of news. America hasn't had a lopsided presidential contest since 2008, and that had been the first of its kind in a dozen years. With guaranteed high viewership and the country neatly divided into roughly equal red and blue parts, personality-driven coverage of politics in general elections probably wasn't so bad. Coke or Pepsi, Ford or Chevy.

But primary politics are different. That's where the parties are supposed to hash out their ideological differences and agree on the policies they will carry forward into the general election. The idea of the primary election system was that the parties would fight a sort of scrimmage against themselves before moving on to the big game. But for decades, primary coverage has moved toward being more a beauty pageant than a scrimmage.

Remember Professor Lee Ross and the "hostile media effect" experiments that found that different groups could watch identical news reports and each conclude that it was sharply biased against their side and very favorable to the other side. Imagine how those perceptions would spike if the participants had been stewing in partisan media beforehand. Now that partisans can marinate in affirmations around the clock online and on TV, even fair questioners would sound like Torquemada. It would be good for potential nominees to be put through their paces before they got to the general election, so it would therefore be in the parties' interests to encourage fair, disinterested debates rather than pep rallies. Plus, the latter are more likely to produce candidates who take extreme positions that might weigh down the eventual nominee in the fall. But like Congress, the two major political parties are now too weak to offer much resistance.

---

The consumers of partisan news must believe that it is good for their preferred parties' chances, or else why would they use it?

According to a 2020 Pew Research Center report, 95 percent of Americans who identified MSNBC as their primary source of political news said they were Democrats or leaned that way.[22] Ninety-three percent of those who put Fox News first identified themselves as Republicans or Republican leaners. The *New York Times* broke 91 percent for the blue team.

Like the respondents to that goofball *New Republic* mailer who must think that buying a subscription to a left-wing magazine really does something to stop the "right-wing crazies," the viewers and readers of the big partisan outlets may be there for a lot of things—belongingness, entertainment, "the joy of hate," as one cable host described it, heck, even information—but they surely must believe that they are helping the cause, not just the clicks and ratings.[23] This is the trap where the parties find themselves. All this friendly coverage is killing the organizations where the actual work is supposed to be getting done.

There are a lot of reasons that American political parties are so perniciously weak. The double whammy of the 2002 McCain-Feingold campaign spending law and then the 2010 *Citizens United* Supreme Court decision put fundraising for the Democratic National Committee and the Republican National Committee on the canvas. The law was supposed to redirect contributions away from "soft money" given to the parties that could be deployed at party leaders' discretion and toward "hard money" that had to be applied to a specific campaign. When the Supreme Court ruled that the obviously unconstitutional provisions in the law limiting how and when outside groups could spend their money to express their own views, it was a nightmare for both parties. Donors could avoid the campaign contribution disclosure and caps and just fund super PACs and independent expenditures.

Since these groups don't tend to carry institutional objectives beyond winning the next election, questions about how the money is spent, which candidates get resources, or whether the message fits with the party brand often go unanswered. Like the celebrity members of Congress, many of the outside groups are not there to strengthen the institution, but to achieve a win—or at least a fat cut of the contributions for themselves.

However, perhaps nothing has hurt the parties as much as the rise of siloed media. As you'll see more in the next chapter, negative, personality-driven partisanship works wonders for #content but tends to hollow out parties that are supposed to do important work in deciding which issues are the proper focus for their members, candidates, and elected officials. It seems that parties are increasingly pursuing the issues set by the media outlets most popular with their voters. But like I said, good politics is often bad TV.

How long did MSNBC and the *New York Times* push the "defund the police" message in 2020 before it occurred to most Democrats that this was a very terrible campaign issue? Viewers and readers in tight ideological clusters may have eaten it up, but it almost cost Joe Biden the White House.

Fox News and much of the rest of the right-side news media have been doing something similar to Republicans on the issue of the January 6, 2021, attack on the U.S. Capitol. There are probably tons of viewers and readers who love the narrative about the "false flag" conspiracy to set up Trump supporters. But what the 93 percent Republican hard-core audience likes is not the same as what will help Republican candidates win in November. The *last* thing Republicans should be doing is trying to defend or excuse the attack on the Capitol or Trump's effort to steal a second term. Not only do those things distract from more persuasive messages, but the party's inability to put those disasters behind it tells swing voters that the GOP is still messed up on kookism. When the RNC passed a censure resolution against Representatives Liz Cheney and Adam Kinzinger for serving on the House January 6 Committee, it was a near-perfect expression of the revered roles of the press and the parties. The resolution won't win any votes in a midterm race, and may even cost some. But while the right wing set the agenda, the party served up clickbait.

If anybody ever tells you that Fox News is a tool of the Republican Party, show them the clip of Senator Ted Cruz of Texas on *Tucker Carlson Tonight* on the one-year anniversary of the Capitol attack. Cruz came on the show to beg forgiveness for having referred to the riot as "a violent terrorist attack on the Capitol." The attack was aimed at causing terror in furtherance of a political goal, so Cruz was right, strictly speaking. But he was still a quavery mass of regret and humiliation as he begged forgiveness for his departure from Carlson's line that the attack will provide the excuse for the persecution of all nationalists and other right-wingers. By using the t-word, Cruz had played right into the hands of the enemy.

Again, this is not a good topic at all for Republicans if they want to win Congress back. Every day that the attack or Trump's effort to steal a second term is big news is a day that the main story isn't about the many woes of Biden and the Democrats. But that's an everyday problem for Republicans caused by right-wing media. Democrats had "defund the police"; now Republicans have "legitimate political discourse."[24] More telling, though, was Carlson's treatment of Cruz.

After Cruz had gotten finished with his auto-da-fé, Carlson came back even harder: "You told that lie on purpose, and I'm wondering why you did." The segment went on for nine excruciating minutes as the host of Republicans' favorite news outlet humiliated a Republican senator over an issue that is poison for the party. Even given Cruz's superhuman capacity to endure humiliation in pursuit of power, it was hard to watch.

That doesn't sound like "A Plan for Putting the GOP on TV News" that Roger Ailes pitched to Richard Nixon in 1970 and then brought to life twenty-five years later.[25] It sounds more like a party that has been captured by an enterprise that does not share its same goals.

# 5.

## OUTSOURCING OUR MORALITY
### How Personality-Driven Coverage
### Leads to Nihilism

*I'm not just an entertainer! I'm an influencer, a wielder of*
*opinion. A force!*

—Lonesome Rhodes, played by Andy Griffith in the 1957 film
*A Face in the Crowd,* written by Budd Schulberg

On December 15, 2021, the *Washington Post* made a startling declaration in a headline: "Climate change has destabilized the Earth's poles, putting the rest of the planet in peril."[1] To a person not familiar with the way American journalism works these days, this would seem like a stop-the-presses, whoa-Nellie kind of revelation.

The subhead made it seem even more so: "For the first time this year, rain fell on the summit of the Greenland ice sheet. Beavers and commercial ships are invading formerly frozen areas. A crucial Antarctic ice shelf is on the brink of collapse. New research shows how rising temperatures have irreversibly altered both the Arctic and Antarctic. The ripple effects will be felt around the globe."

Irreversible global ripples! Crucial collapse! Invading beaver!

But on the *Post*'s home page, the story played below a couple of incremental items on the January 6 attack—a potential subpoena for the former White House chief of staff and civil suits against some of the participants—and the account by one of the *Post*'s politics reporters of her own journey to better understand her physicist grandmother, famous for her work on the atomic bomb sixty-five years before.[2] If the beavers are invading and the "rest of the planet [is] in peril," why is the *Post* putting the story below worthwhile but incremental news and an indulgent first-person account from one of its own reporters?

Any experienced news consumer knows the game. Stories about, literally, the end of the world are there to provide the thrum that provides the backdrop for the rest of everything else. You can't exactly tell readers, viewers, or listeners that the end is really nigh and then offer the latest on Mark Meadows's testimony or the memoirs of physicists' granddaughters. What you can do, though, is at regular intervals remind consumers that our way of life or even life itself is in crisis, that the crisis is probably irreversible and that they should despair—but slowly, and after they read "Ask Carolyn."

The *Post* even innovated a unique way to profit from this below-the-fold existential dread. The paper partnered in 2019 with Rolex (presumably income inequality coverage was not a good fit) to offer a new section called Climate Solutions that looks at the bright side of our imminent, irreversible demise. Some typical headlines: "From novelist to climate crusader: How one woman is working to put a stop to natural gas," "Pets can help fight climate change with an insect-based diet. Owners just need to come around to the idea," and "A harvest for the world: A Black family farm is fighting racism in agriculture and climate change."[3]

The *WaPo* and Rolex were trying to show that slowing the demise of life as we know it can be both fun and profitable. It's a kind of common worldview in upper-caste America, Britain, and elsewhere in the West. It's as if the planet and our species are in hospice and about the best we can do is try to stay comfortable. And if along the way we advance ourselves and our allies, then the journey will have been its own reward.

Yes, the beavers have invaded the ice sheets of Greenland, and soon will overrun our positions here, but what better way to mark the time until the end than on a new Rolex Submariner?

Whether you think that climate change is an extinction-level event for mankind in the next twenty-five years or are just planning on buying beachfront property in Chattanooga, you know that's a preposterous way to deal with the subject. People with serious views on climate change might appreciate extensive coverage on the subject, but what the coverage cannot be is about a real-live apocalypse that is commingled with a memoir about a reporter's feelings about her grandma and the football scores. So the end of the world has to be treated like Aunt Tilly's cancer diagnosis. We're all very sad about it, but we don't need to cancel our trip to the beach over it. She would have wanted us to go . . .

There are many ways we could describe our era. It is the information age, early-onset idiocracy, the rise of the authoritarians, etc., etc., etc. We won't know the truth until the age is over. But to me, we live in the age of anxiety.

Americans got nearly ten million prescriptions for potent anti-anxiety drugs like Klonopin and Ativan in March 2020. In the same month, there were almost thirty million prescriptions for antidepressants, also often used to combat anxiety. And while the American Psychiatric Association's annual survey found that our worries on a host of subjects retreated in 2021 from all-time highs in 2020, we are way, way more worried compared to the recent past.[4] Many of these worries are intensely personal, but others are dislocated societal or political concerns being experienced as personal anxiety. And that's no good.

There's so much anger in our culture today, and you can't hate something you aren't afraid of. We are an angry people because we are a frightened people. Politicians, popular culture, the news media, and leaders of major institutions speak in a language of anxiety, and did so long before our now-receding pandemic began. It wouldn't be so odd if it weren't for the fact that things are so much better here and now than they've been for most of human existence: freer, richer, safer, cleaner, and easier. Yet somehow endlessly problematic and anxiety-inducing.

There are a lot of reasons for this mismatch. But part is surely a result of media overconsumption—panicky pulp produced to shovel at you in order to hold an audience in a fragmented marketplace. All day, every day, you are offered an unlimited array of serious worries about which you can do next to nothing.

How worried should you be about, say, banana fungus? The story has been everywhere over the past few years, but in case you missed it, the species of bananas that make up almost all human consumption, the Cavendish, is under serious threat. It is the same fungus that took down the previous, ahem, top banana. This time around it could be more serious because of the overreliance on one species. The end of the banana as we know it is a real possibility.

If you live in Ecuador, the world's leading exporter of bananas, you might not be able to help worrying about the Fusarium fungus. Certainly, if you're one of the officials there scanning for funky bananas, you should probably be righteously worried about something that could affect 20 percent of your country's workforce.

What if you live in America? If you work at Chiquita, Dole, or Del Monte, serious concern is merited. The same goes if you work at the Department of Agriculture. You're paid to fret about foreign fungus. But how much should the other 330 million of us worry about banana rot?

Should we worry more than we did about the collapse in honeybee hives a decade ago? That panic was an even bigger smash hit in the doom-pornography branch of journalism than the rotten bananas. The bee alarm proved false, but helped launch untold backyard beekeepers. Now there's a danger that the influx of imported European honeybees for home hives is crowding out better, indigenous pollinators like the all-American bumblebee. So maybe we should worry about that instead. But how much compared to banana blight?

Maybe you're a runner who needs bananas to fight leg cramps. Maybe you have a little one new to solid foods who basically subsists on a diet of bananas and little star-shaped rice puffs. Maybe you have reservations at Brennan's. Let's just say you like bananas enough to worry about disruptions. Fine. But at what cost to the other worries you're already nurturing?

Will bananxiety take away from your concern about space junk? The seagrass collapse that's killing manatees in Florida? Cryptocurrency wealth inequality? The cooling of the sun? The return of capes to men's fashion? These are all bad things; some may be even worse than living in a world of banana blight. But if you think of the banana problem as part of something larger— climate change, the exploitation of workers in poor countries, global trade, etc.—you can probably make room for some concern.

But what about your real fears? Big things mostly out of your control: the corrosion of our system of government, the environment, the economy, etc. The big things in your own life: your relationships, your career, your diet, that weird bump or lump you noticed, your kids, your parents. . . . Banana fungus can't compete with those things because they really are your responsibility.

You don't want to be oblivious, though, so maybe just put it in the pile of stimulus-response anxieties. Every time you see the banana bin at the front of the produce section or watch a Minions movie with your kids, you can check the boxes: You know what the problem is and you care about it, and you can nod gravely about it when someone brings it up at Pilates. And there banana fungus can, excuse me, rot, along with man capes, space trash, the solar minimum, seagrass, ineffective pollinators, and the Bitcoin divide. Like a stack of unanswered mail, the possibility of a banana panic can wait for its turn to rob you of a little piece of mind.

Piling up the unpaid bills of worry creates problems for us personally, yes. But it also is behind our nation's serious collective-action problem. Obsessive concern about problems mostly beyond our control can prevent us from taking action on the ordinary, important work institutions are supposed to do. If the spending bill is really the last hope of a dying planet, then we can't have the right conversation about how much to spend and for how long. Overhyped anxiety also distracts us. If you're running a "forensic audit" looking for ballot boogeymen, you can't do your job as a state official. Exaggerated, dislocated anxieties, even when sincere, are keeping us from our real work.

Then there's burnout. In an era where everything is a crisis, then nothing really is one. How many overhyped panics do we expect Americans to endure before reaching the rational conclusion that the news media, their politically addicted peers, and institutional leaders have lost all perspective? The boy who cried wolf is clogging your Facebook feed with global warming or vaccine memes and hollering about murder hornets on TV. The next step is to pop a Xanax and tune out.

We hear constantly about the need to "raise awareness," but in the age of anxiety, all this awareness is proving paralytic. We'd all do better to try to live our lives and let the bananas fall where they may.

That doesn't mean that there might not be a banana crisis. Or a climate crisis. Or a democracy crisis. Or a decency crisis. Or an education crisis. Or a mental health crisis. Or a debt crisis. Or an obesity crisis. Or whichever of the dozens of problems we hear are emergent, dire, and demanding our full attention. Because the next week or month or year will make all the difference. Remember: *This* is the most important election of all time . . .

But as Roger Ailes once said of Glenn Beck after the departure of the zany apocalyptist from Fox News, "The problem with predicting the end of the world every day is that sooner or later, you have to deliver."

Especially because reporters and the outlets where they work tend to overstate the severity of the problems they cover, issue-oriented news tends to be pretty depressing. It goes against the business model of most news outlets as well as human nature to tell audiences, "Don't worry too much about it, but here's a story you might be interested in." If you want people to click your link or not change the channel, you have to make the story compelling. Alas, the easiest way to make a boring story compelling is to exaggerate the potential consequences. The cumulative effect is for news consumers to despair and ultimately tune out completely.

That's why you need to keep the apocalypse low-key and available for sponsorships. It's back there providing that thrum, but also imparting legitimacy to the rest of what you're doing. Here's where journalists perform a neat bit of legerdemain. They turn their coverage of serious news into the idea that they themselves are serious people who should be afforded respect. By this trick, an overcoiffed, undereducated newsreader can demand you treat them as credible even when they are talking to an imbecilic pop star about their big breakup announcement on Instagram because in the previous segment the talking head was talking about war, pestilence, and plague.

It's an important trick, because it's the fluff that is the lowest-risk, highest-reward infotainment of all. To use the jargon of news consultants, it's about "humanizing" the news. That's great if you are trying to help readers, listeners, or viewers understand how a story might affect them personally. But most of the humanization goes in the other direction: away from ideas and toward the personification of all things. It's good to make ideas understandable on a human scale to news consumers, but bad to anthropomorphize concepts into individual politicians. That usually means talking less about policies and more about personalities.

Think about the long, long discussion in President Biden's first year about progressive Democrats' proposed social welfare and environmental spending package, initially floated at $6 trillion. I can't tell you the actual split on policy coverage versus personality coverage, but I imagine a lot more people learned that Senator Joe Manchin has a snazzy boat on the Potomac River than learned the significant details of the legislation he opposed. The story so many outlets told about a coal-state senator blocking legislation that was said to be very good for the climate was an easy sell, shifting effortlessly into *why* Manchin would do such a mean thing. Was he corrupt or just cynical? Little considered was the possibility that he actually believed what he was saying. You have a bad guy, the heroes trying to overcome him, and that ever-present, low-key doomsday providing the juice.

Here's how *Politico*'s White House editor, Sam Stein, reacted when Manchin said he would not back the bill: "A lot to process on the Manchin news but, from a substantive standpoint, it's just objectively devastating for the planet," Stein tweeted. "The last best chance at climate change legislation is gone."[5] That's quite a thing for one person to accomplish, devastating the whole planet by opposing $500 billion in new spending on green energy over the next decade. Manchin sounds more like a supervillain than one of one hundred senators. It's nonsense, but it's easier to sell than the boring, incremental truth.

The world is ending and your bananas are in peril, and you really can't do much of anything about it. But here is a savior who could protect you or a devil who is trying to hasten the Four Horsemen. This kind of coverage invites you to watch from the stands as these avatars of good and evil clash.

It's no surprise that personality-driven coverage attracts and rewards all of the wrong sorts of politicians.

---

To be an offensive coordinator in the National Football League is a pretty sweet gig. Salaries at top-drawer teams go well above $1 million a year, and if you can handle pressure, it's an exciting job with the chance to one day be a head coach making $10 million or more.[6]

But to do the job, you must accept that there will be a little camera installed in the booth where you work during games, just to the left of your monitor. When your play fails, that camera will go live, beaming the most unattractive view possible of your double chin and nostrils to millions of fans at home. You must be able to absorb your failure and move ahead to the next play without becoming distracted by the fact that how you react will be part of your public identity and, by extension, your prospects for future success. You'd better keep cool or show the right kind of performative anger.

This certainly must be bad for the work of offensive coordinating. It usually isn't good to have people wondering too much about "optics" while doing their jobs. But it makes good TV, and the NFL is primarily a television show. If it helps ratings to show the world the reddened face of the guy getting blamed for the botched drive, then this little cruelty is in service of the larger goal. The coordinators know it and probably can't help but practice their looks and responses *Zoolander*-style in the mirror on game day.

What if ratings aren't the point, though? What about nostril cams then?

If you want to know, just turn on almost any congressional hearing and watch supposed adults bark like seals to be thrown their fish: five minutes of camera time in which they can try to manufacture some "moment" that is believed to be helpful in the thing that always matters most in Washington: getting reelected. Watch especially for the habit of members who have the temerity to not attend the whole session, but arrive in time to ask a usually even more obtuse version of what has already been asked many times. Politicians will go to humiliating lengths to have cameras shoved at them and then do it all over again.

News coverage affects outcomes in many areas. We often see stories about a "controversial" issue, the controversy for which is provided by the coverage itself. "Many questions tonight about the controversial decision." Indeed. The questions and the controversy are generated by reporters. That's bad enough, but reporters often enlist social media posts to reinforce the perception of conflict.

We all know the life cycle: A politician looking for attention says something inflammatory; rival politicians and other social media scavengers deliver the intended response of outrage and indignation. "Sen. Joe Schmo just said he wants to ban lemonade stands" begets "Schmo's anti-kid legislation gets DESTROYED." But the circle be unbroken: Up next is "Schmo haters beclown themselves with unhinged attacks" and "Why the Schmo plan is actually good for kids." The senator got all he wanted for the cost of simply saying or proposing something controversial. The doomed legislation earns him attention through the hatred of his detractors and the counterattacks by his own core supporters.

For instance, this is a real headline in *The Hill*: "Judiciary hearing ERUPTS as Mazie Hirono tells Ted Cruz to stop 'MANSPLAINING.'"[7] Not that it mattered, but the hearing was for a judicial nominee. First, the hearing most certainly did not "erupt" in any even figurative sense of the word. Cruz was trying to trip up the nominee into contradicting Hirono. Cruz ran long and was told to stop talking by the senator leading the meeting, Democrat Jon Ossoff of Georgia. Cruz, on cue, took umbrage. Then Hirono took her turn, and threw in the lame "mansplaining" zinger. The question was pointless, the argument was useless, and, almost one million views later, it succeeded only as a way to wring some clicks out of what was a perfunctory hearing.

It would be like the offensive coordinators sending in lunatic plays in hopes of keeping the camera on them as much as possible. Donald Trump took the obvious next step of just moving a

few boxes down in the stadium and sitting right in the broadcast booth. At some point in the past twenty years, we went from
politicians pursuing coverage in the name of raising awareness
for legislation or a campaign to today, when the coverage is itself
the point.

We are left with a media ecosystem that helps politicians stay
in power and creates profit for individuals without ever producing anything useful for anybody else. Cruz and Hirono are doing
the same thing, just from opposite ends of the field. And if one
of their putative teammates decides to try legislation instead of
manipulation, that can be turned into more outrage. Smart,
well-educated people who surely must have once imagined being
real lawmakers end up as players in a game of Pong, volleying
their umbrage back and forth but never getting anything done.

In order to keep up with lesser intellects who are more willing to debase themselves to be famous, smart lawmakers who
know American political history are willing to play along. If
Matt Gaetz and Ilhan Omar can become household names without ever accomplishing anything, who wants to be serious about
legislating?

It is among the most pernicious problems in our era of
dysfunctional government and politics. The people who are willing to do what it takes to be famous enough to win office are
increasingly unsuitable custodians of power. People of good judgment and decency who are unwilling to have a camera pointed
up their nostrils day and night increasingly cannot win elective office. We turned politics into a reality show and got reality
show–caliber politicians.

Most desirable traits of leadership are consistent across nations
and cultures: decency, fairness, and the ability to inspire can all be
good things whether you live in an authoritarian nation or a liberal

democracy. In fact, the more powerful the form of government, the more important those virtues are. The reason we reject concentrated authority in the United States is that our national project is based on the understanding of human nature as self-seeking and prone to the abuse of power. If a position has such power that it should only admit women and men of extraordinary character, then we should have extraordinarily few such positions; and even then set watchmen in the other branches of government.

But the limiting and division of power doesn't lessen the need for virtuous leadership; it only emphasizes different virtues. A monarch or a dictator might need extraordinarily good ethics and compassion to be a virtuous leader. They might also need large doses of charisma and the ability to form a strong emotional connection with their subjects. In a republic, though, it is the other way around. We can make accommodations for the human capacity for corruption and cruelty. America has had lots of corrupt and cruel people in very senior positions in our government over time. Mostly, their rottenness has been contained and sometimes is even punished.

Again, this is not to say that venality and selfishness aren't bad things, only that they can more easily be hedged in a working constitutional system. While Donald Trump certainly did real damage to the constitutional order—we won't know how much at least until our next presidential election is over—it is more remarkable how much the system was able to constrain him. A leader of Trump's greed and enthusiastic ignorance could have brought down an empire if he were a king. As president, though, he was mostly limited to a lot of talk. Most presidents end up yearning for the kind of power enjoyed by the maximum rulers of the world in places like Russia and China. Trump did so nakedly, while many of his predecessors, like Barack Obama, also spoke openly of the advantages of centralized power. Their yearning itself would be sufficient evidence for why we keep it from them.

If resistance to corruption is less important in a constitutional system than it is in a system of centralized authority, it goes the other way, too. What is a virtue in a king may quickly become a vice for a leader in a republic, and that is certainly the case with the manipulation of public opinion. A ruler needs a powerful, reliable emotional connection with his or her subjects. When the people at the top make the decisions for everyone, they had better be able to at least manufacture support.

In a constitutional democracy, though, charisma can be a dangerous thing. The basic project of our Constitution was to find a way for Americans to govern themselves without charismatic leaders turning democracy into mob rule, as would happen in the French Revolution, which began the year after our national charter was ratified. The need for the effective governance the Constitution would provide, argued Alexander Hamilton in *Federalist* No. 1, was that liberty could not survive chaos.

When a government cannot provide basic protections and services for individuals, individuals will demand a government that can. In a democracy, the contest then is between those calling for restraint and those calling for radical change, the latter being very attractive to voters in times of crisis. The ones who come as champions of the people therefore have an obvious advantage in politics over those calling for fairness, order, and dispassion. History told Hamilton, as it still tells us today, about those "paying an obsequious court to the people." He sees them "commencing [as] demagogues, and ending [as] tyrants."

The Constitution provides fire breaks against such men and women by setting limits on individual power and distributing it across three federal branches and down to states. But since

the start, American politicians have worked to accrete power for themselves, usually by obsequiously courting public opinion. With the beginning of the era of mass media, that has always meant trying to manipulate news coverage.

This brings us to the next bit of tension in the American experiment. One way to try to prevent aspiring tyrants from using the press to mobilize mobs would be to set limits on the press. That's a trade-off that other democracies have made, but not one that was acceptable to the participants of a revolution that had been well served by newspapers and who deeply resented the restrictions on free speech from their former mother country. As we talked about at the start of this book, there was no way the Founders were going to risk a royal-style system abridging freedom of speech or of the press.

Even if we hadn't built in such hard restrictions against government regulation of the news from the start, I would still advocate the same kinds of First Amendment protections for the press today. We'll touch on this again in the closing chapters as we discuss the ways forward from here for producers and consumers of news, but the risk of abuse of power remains as real as ever. I'd still rather have the shambles we've got than risk the evils that might come from a regulated press.

So, what's to keep a free press from being a tool of tyrants rather than an impediment to them? As we saw in our trip through the post–World War II era, the profit motive can help deliver higher-quality content, but not as a default setting. The industry is more than happy to engage in slavish coverage of political figures when that's what the people want, even if it goes against an individual institution's purported bias.

In March 2016, the *New York Times* reported that the campaign of then–Republican front-runner Trump had received nearly $2 billion worth of "earned media"—the term in the communications industry for press coverage.[8] Much of the coverage was sharply negative, but what it may have lacked in tone, it more than made up for in volume. It was six times greater than his closest competitor for the GOP nomination, Senator Ted Cruz of Texas, and more than double that of the Democratic front-runner, Hillary Clinton.

There was no defending the volume of Trump coverage based on news judgment. Trump seldom said anything new, but replayed the same loop of put-downs and bellicosity, only sometimes switching targets, inventing new insults, or trying out different riffs. If news is supposed to be about bringing the latest information to the public, the Trump show was the pits. But as entertainment, it was pure gold.

In the fall of 2015, how could anyone not be transfixed watching Trump ranting about how rival candidate Ben Carson shouldn't be trusted because as a troubled youth, Carson *didn't really* try to stab a man.[9] The bestselling book about the neurosurgeon's unlikely success story tells the tale vividly, but Trump told rally goers in Fort Dodge, Iowa, that Carson was a phony attempted murderer.

"Somebody hits you in the belt, the knife is going in because the belt moves this way," Trump said, dramatically yanking his belt, strutting the stage. "It moves this way. It moves that way. He hit the belt buckle. You want to try it on me? Believe me it ain't going to work. You're going to be successful."

Back before Trump's routine grew stale, the spectacle of a leading presidential candidate simulating a murder onstage as a bunch of upright Iowans sat behind him po-faced was certainly good television. "How stupid are the people of Iowa?" Trump said in exasperation about Carson's recent surge in support. "How stupid are the people of the country to believe this crap?" Don Rickles was still touring back then, but he played casinos, not Fort Dodge. Trump's bawdy, bad-boy act was all the more entertaining because of that context. And the best part was that it hardly had any policy to slow it down. He might call someone "weak" on immigration, but about as far as he got on the issue was the malarkey about a "big, beautiful wall." What a show. Pure personality.

Networks left, right, and center beamed Trump's *Il Duce*–plays–the Strip act from rallies into tens of millions of homes, sometimes multiple times a week. Whether viewers loved him or loved to hate him, they couldn't stop watching. After decades of trying to get presidential candidates to be more entertaining, news outlets finally had an actual entertainer running for president.

John Heilemann and his partner, Mark Halperin, were trailblazers in the moronification of politics for years before Trump arrived. Their gabby, gossipy coverage about the 2008 and 2012 presidential elections was perfect for the fun-sized, personality-driven kind of politics favored by television news. *Double Down*, their book on the 2012 campaign, is to *The Making of the President 1960* as *Entertainment Tonight* is to *See It Now*. Heilemann and Halperin had become the doyennes of the chattering class by managing to be both glib and self-serious at once, the same trick that the hosts of *Morning Joe*, the MSNBC show on which they have both regularly appeared, had perfected.

Trump must have appeared to be a godsend as Heilemann and Halperin struggled to get a new politics unit off the ground for Bloomberg News in 2016. Having reportedly wrested salaries of more than $1 million for their Bloomberg gigs, they needed lots of #content.[10] After years spent trying to turn politicians into media personalities, here was one with a superhuman capacity for personality-driven coverage.

Other candidates agonized over the question of acting undignified in exchange for favorable coverage from Heilemann and Halperin and their ilk. Should Marco Rubio talk about his ankle boots with their "stacked Cuban heel"? Should Hillary Clinton risk spraining her spleen forcing yuks on late-night TV? No trouble there with Trump, whose own view of transactional news coverage lines up pretty closely with the model on which coverage like theirs—a blend of banalities and celebrity-style gossip—was based. Trump gave them clicks and views and they treated him with kid gloves. These were the days when *Morning Joe* cohost Joe Scarborough would brag about his friendship with Trump, a frequent guest, and how he gave the candidate debate advice. "A masterful politician," the former Florida congressman once cooed.[11]

I don't know whether Heilemann and Halperin convinced Trump to ride with them on a Zamboni around Manhattan's Wollman Rink in November 2016, or whether Trump invited them, but ride they did. The three of them bundled together on the back of the ice-cleaning machine while two of America's leading political journalists asked Trump questions like this one: "Here is a question that I've been wanting to ask you for a while: We almost never get to see you eat. What do you like to eat? What's Donald Trump's favorite stuff?"[12] Sweet fancy Moses.

But it got worse. Trump's efforts as a private citizen to save the dilapidated rink in 1986 were at the heart of the mythology the candidate was trying to build as a businessman who could get things done. Dig this:

HALPERIN: People who say Trump's got no experience, he can't possibly be president, because that's not what the president's about, [this ice rink] was a government problem, the city couldn't get this thing built, so what are examples of things now that aren't getting done that you think you could bring the same skills to if you were president, just the way you got this thing done?

TRUMP: I'll give you one example, wars. Wars aren't getting done. It's the same thing.

Even the folks on *Fox & Friends* might have blushed at that kind of question to their friend and frequent guest, Trump. But why was this happening on Bloomberg News, a high-end, mainstream, business-oriented outlet?

In February 2016, Les Moonves, still the head of CBS before being toppled by sexual misconduct allegations, famously summed up the cynically dispatriotic attitude required to perpetuate this kind of sham news coverage: "It may not be good for America, but it's damn good for CBS."[13]

Woof.

"Man, who would have expected the ride we're all having right now? The money's rolling in and this is fun," Moonves told investors at a Morgan Stanley conference in San Francisco. "I've never seen anything like this, and this is going to be a very good year for us. Sorry. It's a terrible thing to say. But, bring it on, Donald. Keep going."[14]

Double woof.

What Moonves & Company loved was the endless personal strife. Campaigns used to be so boring! What could be more dullsville than a couple of oh-so-polite stiffs like Barack Obama and Mitt Romney trading pointed remarks on policy. "The 1980s are now calling to ask for their foreign policy back" was once treated as a killer zinger. Reporters and pundits used to have to really mine for the little nuggets of acrimony they could then refine into pure personality-driven narrative. In 2016, you had a guy comparing one of his opponents to a pedophile and candidates openly arguing about the size of their dingalings.

Why would news executives ever want this kind of personified conflict to stop, even if it means providing the conflict themselves?

In 2021, at another Morgan Stanley event, NewsCorp CEO Lachlan Murdoch was asked about the decline in the Fox News Channel's ratings in the wake of Trump's defeat. He said, no worries, conflict could protect profits.

"The main beneficiary of the Trump administration from a ratings point of view was MSNBC . . . and that's because they were the loyal opposition," Murdoch said. "That's what our job is now with the Biden administration, and you'll see our ratings really improve from here."[15]

Woof again.

If, like Moonves and Murdoch, you don't get too hung up about your own responsibilities beyond the next shareholders' meeting, it makes perfect sense. Even if President Biden, still new in office and fairly popular when Murdoch was speaking, couldn't produce the kinds of intense personal hatred and worship that Trump could deliver just by being himself, Fox could do it for Biden. It didn't matter if the moment had changed or that Trump and Biden were very different; the framing would remain the same.

Not only does the profit model of journalism offer no reliable resistance to the kind of demagogic, personality-driven politics of which the Founders warned, it often acts as an inducement. And it happens even when it is at odds with perceived partisan or ideological leanings, like Trump's Zamboni buddies and CNN's hour after hour of Trump rally coverage. Even when the coverage of Trump from those outlets became relentlessly negative, it still focused far too much on personality than policy. What did Trump say? What did Nancy Pelosi say about what Trump said? What did Kevin McCarthy say about what Pelosi said about what Trump said? What did Sean Hannity say about what Rachel Maddow said about what McCarthy said about what Pelosi said about what Trump said?

This personality-driven claptrap coverage is both a product of and a contributor to the problems we discussed before, particularly in the previous chapter about our collapsing political institutions. There just aren't that many issues of high national salience, certainly not occurring with enough frequency to churn out the volume of coverage required to fill the bottomless pit of major national news outlets. But as has been proven by celebrity and sports news, there is no such thing as *too much* when it comes to personality-driven coverage. The world is ending, you are powerless to stop it, these famous people control your destiny, now smash that like button and stay tuned to see what they say next.

---

In 2020, the Republican Party for the first time in its 164-year history failed to produce a platform for the presidential election. The party began in response to a very specific policy issue, the passage of the Kansas-Nebraska Act, which allowed for the expansion of slavery in the northern territories. The party's founders had to go shopping for a candidate who would carry their banner in 1856, ending up with John Frémont, the western explorer and former Democratic senator from California. In 2020, it went the other way. The candidate would tell the party what it stood for, and the members of the Republican National Committee would stand and salute.

I understand that party platforms are not governing documents, but they are important political texts. They bind candidates to difficult and politically costly positions sought by party members. In exchange, the members agree to limits on their ideological demands, at least through the election. So what does it mean when a party says only this about its preferred policies: that it will "enthusiastically support the President's America-first agenda." The Trump, the whole Trump, and nothing but the Trump, so help them Don.

The RNC cited the coronavirus pandemic and "concern for the safety of convention attendees and [their] hosts" for not gathering to write a platform, but the mass gatherings the party did stage and antagonism of officials in host locations over pandemic rules renders those claims void. The truth was that the platform would be a political liability, either revealing Trump's rejection of core conservative principles or highlighting those points that might prove unpopular with voters. It was a slick political move, but at a high price.

There had been plenty of worshipful treatment of Trump's predecessor, Obama, whose messianic vibes took Democrats even beyond the cult of personality they had fashioned around Bill Clinton sixteen years before. Obama had, as Michael Knox Beran described it, the aura of a shaman to many Democrats: "the Adonis who will turn winter into spring, he revives one of the more pernicious political swindles: the belief that a charismatic leader can ordain a civic happy hour and give a people a sense of community that will make them feel less bad."

While Republicans were certainly guilty of plenty of hero worship with Ronald Reagan, this was the kind of goo-goo stuff that GOPers had mocked in Democrats going back to the Kennedys. That was part of why I initially believed Republicans in 2016 would steer in the other direction and choose the opposite of Obama—experienced, probably a governor or former governor and more yeoman than shaman.

So many members of the GOP had seethed over Obama's king-sized ego, celebrity status, excessive partisanship, and abuses of executive power that I expected them to want the opposite of Obama. The pattern with parties out of power had been well established. Democrats picked the opposite of their perception of George W. Bush in 2008: cerebral, antiwar, and internationalist. Republicans picked the perceived opposite of Bill Clinton in 2000: establishment, plain-spoken, and conservative Christian. Democrats picked the perceived opposite of George H. W. Bush in 1992: young, charismatic, and empathetic. Much the same could be said of the out-party nominees in 1988, 1980, 1976, 1972, 1964, 1960.

It's not that parties make a conscious decision to do the opposite of the president in power. Rather, individuals' sensitivities to vices and virtues are heightened by the most significant stimulus in American political life: the dude who's on television every day. Based on that trend, it made sense that Republicans would abjure the characteristics they saw in Obama and embrace their opposites.

I could blame the incompetent, overfed campaigns of Jeb Bush and Scott Walker or the too-crowded Republican field for my failure in foresight, but the truth is, I underestimated the growing appetite for demagoguery among Republicans and Americans in general. I failed to understand that a significant number of Republicans would want to replicate and intensify the worst characteristics they saw in Obama and unleash them on their enemies: less experience, more ego, ranker partisanship, and pure celebrity. Republicans did not choose an anti-Obama; they chose a mega-Obama.

Yes, Trump was the opposite of Obama in many surficial ways—gaudily jingoistic where Obama was sometimes abashed in his patriotic expressions, old and white instead of young and African American, enthusiastically ignorant rather than professorial—but at the core, Trump was Republicans' answer to Obama, not their alternative.

We have turned every occupant of the Oval Office since at least Richard Nixon into the commanding general of one army in the endless culture war. It's been twenty years since we've had a broadly popular president. This is substantially a function of the nationalization and sorting that we discussed in the previous two chapters, but the effect goes beyond just polarization. We are reversing the direction on the sorting machine. Rather than the parties and partisan leaders reflecting the people, the people are sometimes arranging themselves and their ideas to fit the folks at the top.

Now, we shouldn't pretend that this is wholly new in the American system. From the start, charismatic leaders have left lasting changes on the parties they led and the people in them. Leaders like John F. Kennedy, Franklin Roosevelt, Teddy Roosevelt, Abraham Lincoln, and Andrew Jackson not only shifted the ideologies of their parties, but the personalities of the organizations and their members. And, just as was the case in the time before so much nationalization and polarization, the charisma of leaders is still drawn partly from reflection. People are drawn to exaggerated versions of their own traits. Defenders of both Clinton and Trump, the most solipsistic and ethically feeble of modern presidents, would reliably explain that their misdeeds were those of the common man—or that "anybody" would diddle an intern or use his office for personal gain if given the chance.

Democrats reverted to the historical norm in 2020 and picked the opposite of the vices they perceived in the incumbent, and to my considerable relief, did not seek another demagogic leader. Though President Biden is certainly capable of unnerving degrees of demagoguery—comparing opponents of a suite of Democratic election legislation to the president of the Confederacy, etc.— his candidacy and presidency have been reversions to important norms. Whatever one thinks of his policies and the competency of his administration's execution thereof, Biden has received less obsessive—in ways both favorable and unfavorable—coverage than either of his two immediate predecessors. Biden may be the least charismatic president since the elder Bush, and that's a very welcome change from the deific treatment Obama and Trump received from their followers. One of the best things you can say about the forty-sixth president is that he's kind of boring.

That also means he's bad for business. The stretch from 2015 to 2021 was a bonanza for sellers of news. Starting with Trump's Godzilla attack on the GOP primaries, his stunning upset of Hillary Clinton, and then the Scaramuccian levels of chaos in Trump's administration, including the first of his two impeachments, it was a kind of permanent Christmas for the Moonves-Murdoch set. Then it got better: Trump, plus a once-in-a-century pandemic that forced Americans to stay home, where they could gorge on terrifying news updates. When the 2020 presidential election came along, it was like a second cherry on top of a double fudge sundae. But the first election since Reconstruction when the loser wouldn't concede, followed by the president's goon squad storming the Capitol to try to overturn the results? Pure ambrosia.

The Trump era had delivered far more for the news business than any of them could have dreamed back in the fall of 2015. It may not have been good for America, but it was damn good for CBS/NBC/ABC/Fox/CNN/*WaPo*/*NYT*/etc. But Trump was right when he once warned his frenemies in the press: "Newspapers, television, all forms of media will tank if I'm not there, because without me, their ratings are going down the tubes."[16]

According to the Nielsen company, weekday prime-time viewership in 2021 dropped 38 percent at CNN compared to the previous year, 34 percent at Fox News Channel, and 25 percent at MSNBC.[17] The already beleaguered network evening news took a lashing, too: 12 percent down at ABC and CBS and 14 percent at NBC.

It was the same in the digital world. The *Washington Post*, which had ridden the calamities of the late 2010s to new heights in readership, saw the number of unique visitors to its site slide 44 percent in 2021 compared to one year before, according to ratings from Comscore. The decline was 34 percent for the *New York Times*. And that most treasured attribute for digital outlets, "stickiness," was way down, too. The Associated Press reported that media monitoring company NewsWhip found the average number of engagements—sharing, commenting, etc.—on political articles in 2021 was 321 compared to 924 the year before. Similar data showed commensurate declines in time spent by users on sites.[18]

The high ratings born of a presidential coup attempt in the midst of a global pandemic were never going to be sustainable, but the decline was sharper than industry experts expected. The obvious missing piece is a main character for the personality-driven drama of news. Trump is itching to return to his role as supervillain/savior, but it's not clear that he can still deliver the juice. Republicans still defend their man and a considerable chunk of the party remains absolutely suckered, but the show is pretty stale now. And the others auditioning may have Trump's lack of dignity, but they'll never have his skills of a showman. Ted Cruz or Alexandria Ocasio-Cortez are good for triggering the partisan-outrage feedback loop, but that's no attempted murder simulation at a rally. They're Showtime after 10 p.m. Trump was hard-core.

So maybe we are passing out of the period of greatest danger for the republic. Maybe the events of the previous five years have been terrible enough that Americans are doing for ourselves what the Constitution forbids the government from doing and what the profit motive tends to encourage. News as entertainment is bad for us, and we are consuming less of it. Maybe we can, as we have with junk food, smoking, and other afflictions of affluence, begin to turn a corner. Maybe . . .

The greatest obstacle to our capacity for becoming more responsible consumers of news is moral. And there is quite a lot of energy running against good judgments there.

Some of the members of the Republican National Committee who approved a resolution binding themselves to Trump like serfs to a feudal lord, many of them surely knew it was wrong—not just icky, but wrong. They were intentionally derelicting their duties for the sake of political expediency and broke a noble line going back to the fight to end slavery to do it. In the same way, some of those officials who attended Trump's nomination speech delivered from the White House knew that it was not just unwholesome but un-American to use the people's house that way. I know that, because some of them told me so. The spectacle of Trump using the presidential mansion for a campaign event was bad enough, but he was introduced by his own daughter, whom he had given a high government post. Yuck. As the president was serenaded with an aria from *Turandot*, sung from the Truman Balcony, Trump's name was emblazoned across the Washington Monument in fireworks. This was not just bad taste, but idolatry—a brazen taking of our shared national heritage for political advantage.

The Republicans who knew better didn't say anything about this behavior for the same reason that Democrats didn't speak to the many excesses of the secular religion of antiracism or the suppression of free speech in general. We have become a nation of moral imbeciles in which individuals increasingly outsource their moral reasoning not to their families, religions, or neighbors but to mobs of strangers arranged around obtaining and exercising political power. Cable television, the internet, and social media have collapsed the practical barriers to collective thought and mob action that time and distance formerly provided. Our republican system sets many breaks against the popular tyranny that has been the demise of free peoples throughout time. But none of those barriers was as powerful as the size and diversity of our land and people.

There is no doubt that the abolition of space and time in our communications has had many moral benefits. The birth of national television was a death knell for Jim Crow. Rosa Parks had been a leading figure in organizing black Alabamians for civil rights for more than a decade before her famous arrest in 1955 and the ensuing Montgomery Bus Boycott and protests. That was the same year that the national network news ratings wars truly began, bringing longer shows and more resources; the next year saw the arrival of Chet Huntley and David Brinkley at NBC. It was the physical courage of those who marched in Selma, Alabama, for voting rights in 1965 that inspired the nation in support of their cause. But another development of that year played a part: the introduction of the first evening news broadcasts in color.

Newspaper accounts illustrated with black-and-white photos of the barbarism of the segregationists and the suffering of their victims had been part of news coverage going back to the 1870s. But seeing and hearing this horror from antiquity on the still-revolutionary television—especially in color—was more than the consciences of whites in the North could bear. A considerable part of the genius of Martin Luther King Jr. and the civil rights movement in general was their understanding of the power of television to shame northerners into action.

But we are a long way from that. Now, for all the reasons we've discussed, news coverage is seldom about moral challenge, but rather moral conformity. In an environment where news executives are terrified at the thought of offending viewers, listeners, or readers, who would dare make their audience uncomfortable? Networks took significant risks in showing the scenes from Alabama sixty-five years ago. Some local stations in the segregated South refused to air the evening news and viewers jammed phone lines with calls of protest. Now news outlets call themselves brave for telling audiences exactly what they want to hear.

Tucker Carlson is the host of what is usually one of the two most-watched shows on cable television. He works for a multinational corporation led by an Australian billionaire who owns arguably the single most powerful news outlet in America. Carlson is rich and famous. Yet he regularly rails about the "big, legacy media outlets." Guests denounce the "corporate media" on his show and Fox's CEO calls Carlson "brave" for discussing controversial topics. Yet somehow, nobody even giggles. Carlson and his family have been targeted by kooks and thugs, it's true. It takes courage to keep going in the face of that. But it does not take any kind of journalistic courage to pump out night after night exactly what your audience wants to hear.

Over on MSNBC, host Chris Hayes has made a whole genre out of attacking what he says is the cowardice of Fox and its owners. On any given night, one can tune in to hear about, as he put it in an interview with Ezra Klein, "the most morally disgraceful actions of people in public life in my lifetime is the cynical seeding of vaccine doubts for profit and eyeballs that the right-wing media is engaged in." I made the unfortunate decision once to go on his show to talk about my critiques of cable news. Fine, fine, he said, but he was different from the really bad guys at Fox. "But there are lines," he said. "And there are lines of integrity, and honesty, and I patrol those lines."[19] I was just there to be a palooka for his tough-guy act. If you feel like Colonel Nathan Jessup for maintaining a higher standard of journalism than Carlson and Hannity, maybe set your sights higher. Hayes isn't lying, but he is acting courageous for flooding television screens night after night with comforting, self-confirming pap for his audience.

Ratings—wanting to grow them or fearing their decline—keep news media figures like Hayes and Carlson and their employers in line. And while news coverage certainly helps enforce the tribal boundaries of American public life, social media mobs and the real-life mobs social media can so readily produce have added new fears for those with dissenting points of view. Why did those RNC members who knew better agree to their vassalage? Why do prominent liberals who believe in free speech look at their shoes when people are shouted down or fired for expressing their beliefs? How could so many seemingly normal members of Congress go along with Trump's effort to steal a second term? We know how cable news, the internet, and social media have created an incentive structure for Carlson,

Hayes, Cruz, Ocasio-Cortez, and tens of thousands of others to be more extreme, more outraged, and more negative. But those same media have an effect on the people not courting celebrity-magnifying controversy, too.

"Reason is, and ought only to be the slave of the passions, and can never pretend to any other office than to serve and obey them," wrote philosopher David Hume in his *A Treatise of Human Nature* in 1739. What Hume knew was what evolutionary psychology and neuroscience have tended to confirm: that human beings are amazing rationalizers. Our "passions," or as we might call them, feelings and emotions, are more powerful than our ability to make rational choices. Psychologist Jonathan Haidt has likened the relationship between the two as an elephant with a rider. The rider, reason, can direct the direction of travel as long as it doesn't bother the elephant, our passions. But if the elephant and the rider disagree, it's no question which really has the upper tusk.

Human beings are certainly born with some understanding of natural law—an innate sense of good and bad. But on most issues, we derive our values from our environments starting from birth. The personalities of twins separated at birth might be very similar regardless of different upbringings, but their moral and ethical rules will tend to be a product of their family, culture, faith, and other institutions. This is partly a result of the human instinct to form coalitions and seek acceptance by the groups around us. Humanity's success is owed to our capacity to form tight bonds with not just our families but also strangers and work toward common goals. It's our species' superpower. So our elephants are usually going to drag us toward fitting in with our tribe, and the rational rider on top will figure out a way to explain why it's actually the right thing to do.

"Voting for an infrastructure bill is good and important," says the rider when his party is in power. "The passage of a smaller infrastructure bill is fiscally irresponsible and reckless," says the rider ten months later when his party is out of power. These kinds of flip-flops are as old as politics and driven by the forces Hume identified nearly three hundred years ago. This is why we shouldn't pay much attention to what politicians say about such things. But what happens when those kinds of forces go to work on normal people when it comes to politics?

One of the reasons our Founders put in all those safeguards against those "paying an obsequious court to the people" was that voters are fickle. Take the withdrawal from Afghanistan in 2021. It was wildly popular until it turned into a shambles, at which point it was widely detested. Same for the Iraq invasion. Or look at California's goofball referenda and recall system, where voters can force low taxes and more services at the same time or initiate a recall election of a sitting governor with a relative handful of signatures. But the real goal is to keep the politics part to a minimum. Representative democracy should mean that voters only need to weigh in every couple of years, and the rest of the time they should be free to focus on their own lives.

Now every day brings a new slew of issues on which to have views. People who wish to maintain a decent level of knowledge about public life feel lots of pressure to have strong opinions. If the guy you're watching on TV says that what the guy on the other channel is engaged in is "the most morally disgraceful actions" in four decades, this is not an invitation to think deeply on the news of the day. This is a battle of good and evil, and our elephants know where to lead our riders. And it's not *this idea* versus *that idea*, it is *this person* versus *that person*. And when your opinions on *us* versus *them* will be judged by the entire population of political social media, watch the pachyderms stampede.

With news consumers overwhelmed by an endless catastrophe told and retold by major outlets, those consumers are more likely to take refuge in the simpler narratives of good versus evil and personality-driven coverage. But that decreases the importance of specific issues, which increases the pressure for loyalty to one's group and, most dangerously, the leader of that group. We spent decades listening to complaints about highly ideological politics and how rigid dogmas were preventing compromise. This was the common trope of the 1990s and 20-aughts. There was some truth to the charge, but I did note that it was usually offered as an attack on the other side of the accuser. Even so, purity tests for ideology can be a bad thing if taken beyond anything but first-order concerns. Extremism in defense of liberty is indeed no vice, but how about in the highway bill markup? What we have now, though, are too many purity tests for loyalty. And if issues don't matter, obedience matters too much.

So, where does that leave us? The profit motive won't serve as a guard against those "commencing [as] demagogues, and ending [as] tyrants" in any reliable way. The Constitution forbids regulation of the press, and our recent experiences with would-be authoritarians suggest this was a wise proscription. So, what are we to do? Like the Americans before us who had to adapt to the telegraph, telephone, radio, television, and cable, we are going to have to become better consumers so we can become better citizens. But before we get to how you can do your part to fight tyranny (and improve your own quality of life), let's talk about how the conscientious members of my profession can be better roadblocks to the march toward mob rule.

# 6.

## POST-JOURNALISM OR ASPIRATIONAL FAIRNESS?
### How to Build a Better News Business

*The world is in a mess*
*With politics and taxes*
*And people grinding axes*
*There's no happiness.*

—George Gershwin, "Slap That Bass," sung by Fred Astaire
in the film *Shall We Dance*, 1938

O ne of the ways that journalism has gotten into such a pickle is the mistaken belief among the members of my vocation that our generation and our problems are fundamentally different from the ones that came before us.

As we've already seen with the partisan press of the early 1800s, the rise of radio propagandists, and the shift from written to broadcast news, there have been similar, if not more serious, predicaments before. But that's not how it feels when you're in it—when it's your newspaper that closes, when it's you who gets fired, when it's you who is the target of the online mob.

I've been in all of those places, and I understand the appeal of apocalypticism, but just as with politics, that kind of thinking is an invitation to error and radicalism at exactly the moment when what is most needed is rigor and steadiness.

One way is toward "post-journalism," the term media scholar Andrey Miroshnichenko coined to describe the move "away from even aspirational fairness and balance and towards shared anger and the powerful emotional connections it can create."[1] The other way is back toward the very concepts that post-journalism rejects.

In our concluding chapter, we will look at what news consumers need to do for their own sakes and for the country. But in this chapter, I want to speak directly to my fellow journalists about some very practical ways I think we can better serve our audiences as well as the culture and country we love.

You don't have to love America or revere our system to be a journalist. It is a free country, after all. But for most of us, it is essential to understand our work in the context of good citizenship and civic responsibility. What we do is not an abstraction, but rather an essential service to facilitate the free flow of ideas and information to allow for both voters and those in positions of authority to make better decisions. If we do our jobs well, we deepen the bonds between Americans themselves and with our noble national project of government for, of, and by the people. If we do our jobs poorly, we create enmity between Americans and toward our common purpose.

Post-journalism rejects the idea of our work being attached to the broad ideas of the Founding and the national interest and is instead focused on satisfying the intense feelings of a narrow but loyal consumer base. Here's how Miroshnichenko describes it:

The business model, predominantly based on ad revenue and large profits, predefined the method of agenda-setting. Generally, the mainstream media's journalism facilitated consumerism, political stability, and the populace's alignment with the policies of the elites, as these were the necessary conditions for the successful application of that business model. Buoyed by this economic foundation, the media also carried out a public service, supporting democracy as a political mode of capitalism.

Within the space of a mere twenty years, the internet completely broke the idyll, which had taken about five hundred years to build. The consequences have gone far beyond just the switch of the material carrier and the ensuing death of newspapers. As the social, economic, and technological conditions that brought about journalism are fading, so is journalism. What remains of it has begun mutating.[2]

This is the world of Alex Jones's InfoWars, the ironically named One America News, and the *New York Times*' 1619 Project: content not only detached from reality but from the concept of any shared purpose for all Americans. Rather than appealing to a broad audience with reliable information and a balanced approach, it offers a bespoke reality for a narrow, intense customer base.

Remember George Orwell writing about the news coverage of the Spanish Civil War and the rise of fascism across Europe: "I know it is the fashion to say that most of recorded history is lies anyway. I am willing to believe that history is for the most part inaccurate and biased, but what is peculiar to our own age is the abandonment of the idea that history could be truthfully written."[3] Not just your age, Mr. Orwell.

"Origin stories function, to a degree, as myths designed to create a shared sense of history and purpose," writes Nikole Hannah-Jones to open the final chapter of *The 1619 Project: A New Origin Story*, a book-length version of the 2019 *New York Times Magazine* series that asserted that the true founding of

America was the arrival of African slaves in Virginia the year before the Pilgrims arrived at Plymouth.[4]

Certainly, every superhero-loving six-year-old knows "origin stories" are important. If we didn't know about the murder of his parents, Bruce Wayne would seem like a rich weirdo in a rubber suit. Hannah-Jones says that America's story—the one that connects the freedom-loving colonists to the American creed of the Declaration of Independence to Abraham Lincoln's Gettysburg Address to Martin Luther King's speech at the Lincoln Memorial—has harmed her and other black Americans. The "erasure," as she called it in one recent interview, of the start of slavery from our national story has been evidence "of how history is shaped by people who decide what's important."[5] In his introduction, the book's editor, Jake Silverstein, says that the aim of the project, which now also includes this weighty tome, a children's book, and a podcast, is no less than "to reframe American history, making explicit that slavery is the foundation on which this country is built." Oh. Is that all?

Perhaps understanding how arrogant such an ambition sounds, and no doubt still smarting from the embarrassment of the gross historical failures of the project at its start, the book is kitted out with the trappings of scholarly work, including a kind of intramural peer review process and piles of footnotes that take the collection past six hundred pages.[6] It still never quite explains how "slavery is the foundation on which this country is built," but it certainly takes dead aim at King's idea of the "promissory note" of America's founding that has for decades been at the center of our national identity.

Hannah-Jones takes on the task of trying to create what she says will be the "shared sense of history" to which the book aspires. The result was a lot of defensive-sounding finger-wagging in response to the historians that had punctured the project's initial premise that Americans rebelled against King George III because they wanted to protect legal slavery. For example, she cites an offer to slaves by British forces during the Revolutionary War for freedom in exchange for military service. But the revolution had already begun, so what's her point? That it made Virginians very angry, and that our most important founders were from Virginia so . . . you know . . . it was a big deal.

Rather than absorbing the response from historians and returning with a more thoughtful and inclusive approach, like the one offered by *Times* music critic Wesley Morris in his revised essay, Hannah-Jones dismisses even the gentle reproaches of her kindest critics and barrels forward.[7]

Dorm room denizens beneath halos of bong smoke would be embarrassed to offer such insights as Hannah-Jones, but she is perhaps the most acclaimed journalist of her generation: a Pulitzer Prize, a MacArthur Foundation genius grant, and a Peabody Award, just for openers. Having been affirmed by the intellectual establishment every step of the way, even when she was preposterously wrong, Hannah-Jones is not going to just suddenly develop humility and circumspection.

When she returns some three hundred pages later to offer her summation, Hannah-Jones is ready to tell you what your new sense of purpose should be. The book that tries to pass itself off as a serious history closes with a political call to action, including "a livable wage; universal healthcare, childcare, and college; and student loan debt relief" as well as reparations payments to everyone who can "trace at least one ancestor back to American slavery."[8]

If you do not agree or you have not absorbed this new "shared sense of history and purpose," guess what you are? "[You] now have reached the end of this book, and nationalized amnesia can no longer provide the excuse," she writes. "None of us can be held responsible for the wrongs of our ancestors. But if today we choose not to do the right and necessary thing, *that* burden we own." You, the heathen, are still a racist if you do not see the light after reading the sacred text.

This is post-journalism in its uncut form. It divides the world into good people and bad people and profits by the intense feelings those divisions generate. The 1619 Project is a particularly effulgent example because its stated purpose is to destroy the idea of the American Creed. It is little different than Fox News suggesting that the January 6 attack was a "false flag" operation intended to provide a pretext to put patriotic nationalists in a prisoner of war camp.[9]

The *New York Times* is using a frontal assault on the idea of America's founding as a new birth of freedom that it very plainly, if imperfectly, was in order to upsell super-users from subscriptions to thirty-five-dollar books.[10] Fox is inciting black-helicopter level paranoia and hatred to get viewers of its free cable news channel to sign up for a sixty-five-dollar "Patriot" package on its subscription streaming service.[11]

This is the world of post-journalism that Miroshnichenko foresees. Deprived of their ability to make large profits by controlling access to information, media companies will turn into commanders in the culture war.

"Having lost the ability to commodify news downwards and agenda upwards, the media have found a last-ditch solution— selling agenda downwards," Miroshnichenko writes. "Under the validation fee, foundation funding, the membership model and its subscription-like surrogates, the media are paid seemingly from below; however, they are not paid for news, but for agenda-setting—for the reasons and motives normally coming from above.

"This hybrid business model leads journalism to mutate into activism and the media to transform into the means of crowd-sourced propaganda. Instead of manufacturing consumerism and consent, the media manufacture polarization and anger."[12]

Rather than rejecting this model, too many journalists are embracing it as a virtue.

The argument against "bothsidesism" and artificial balance and in favor of chucking objectivity for a new kind of activist journalism is understandable. Poor and marginalized people *do* lack representation in coverage. Real moral imbalances *are* sometimes hidden under he-said-she-said kinds of coverage. Reporters, editors, and producers continue to make false equivalencies, consciously or unconsciously, in ways that serve an agenda. "Whataboutism" is an endless rabbit hole down which almost any story with a political element can be flung.

But at the very moment when Miroshnichenko's ominous prophecy is becoming reality, we have a deep obligation to our audience and our country to fight for journalism that can unite instead of divide.

The qualifier "aspirational" that Miroshnichenko puts in front of the word "fairness" speaks to some hard truths that we have had to confront about the limits of objectivity—the ones mentioned above in this chapter, but also in our discussions of implicit bias, fundamental attribution error, and thick bubbles. But "aspirational fairness" also speaks to some misconceptions about the idea of objectivity itself.

Our understanding of journalistic objectivity was the result of a consensus born out of World War II, in which journalists were anything but unbiased. They marched in uniform and submitted their copy to censors in the name of the war effort. In 1945, ten years after reporter Robert Geiger gave the world the term "Dust Bowl," he was just off the coast of Iwo Jima as his Associated Press colleague, photographer Joe Rosenthal, snapped the famous picture of the Marines raising Old Glory atop Mount Suribachi.[13] But the picture we love and is the basis for the Marine Corps War Memorial at Arlington National Cemetery was the *second* flag raising, not the initial one, carried out under more dangerous conditions.[14] But who could blame Rosenthal or the Marines for wanting a better shot, given the unimaginable horrors they had endured in capturing the island and in honor of the many men who laid down their lives?

But the vocation that Geiger, Rosenthal, Ernie Pyle, Edward R. Murrow, and Walter Cronkite shaped when they returned from war coverage aimed at a kind of perfect impartiality that would have been unfamiliar during the conflict or before it. This was the birth of modern, professional, systematized journalism, and it turned out to be like a lot of things we attempted to systematize in the middle decades of the previous century. What it offered in uniformity did not compensate entirely for a lack of flexibility and the creation of "both sides" loopholes in which scoundrels could hide.

The idea of perfect objectivity to which reporters aspired and journalism schools taught proved impossible to achieve in reality. But that does not mean we should not *aspire* to fairness and balance. There are many virtues in life that are impossible to perfectly achieve, but yet are still worth pursuing. Americans need more common spaces in which they can have confidence not only that information will be accurate, but that points of view will be fairly represented. We will always come up short in our inclusivity, impartiality, and capacity for holding bad actors to account, but if we throw away aspirational fairness in favor of activist, opinionated journalism we are not fighting entrenched power, but feeding it.

Post-journalism can turn a reporter's rebellion against traditional norms into profits wrung out of our decaying consensus. America needs journalists committed to her principles and who take seriously our obligation to facilitate useful discourse in a healthy republic. That is the only counterweight I can think of to fight the crushing cynicism of our post-journalistic future. Civic duty has to be our organizing principle.

American journalism cannot exist in a space detached from the mission of the nation that proclaims and protects the right to free expression. Our rights as journalists do not exist apart from the other natural rights described in our Founding, but rather are inseparable from them. The free press doesn't even get its own amendment, but is in a bundle with religion, speech, peaceable assembly, and the right to petition the government. The first appropriate bias beyond the ones toward humanity itself and against dishonesty in our work should be in favor of the system that protects us and our vocation. This should never be a matter of partisanship, but an attachment to the idea that the Constitution provides the correct means by which Americans should resolve their disputes and that the goals laid out in the Declaration of Independence are the rightful aims of our government. Americanism is an antidote to post-journalism.

I am in no position to offer any lectures on journalism beyond what my own experience has taught me, quite often as a result of my own mistakes. I have no academic credentials and, frankly, have no regrets about that. Journalism is a worthy subject for academic inquiry, and I am glad that there are so many studying the industry and its craft. But for working reporters, I have too often seen academic expectations crash and burn in real-world settings. I advise those who want specialized training in this vocation to only do so *after* finding someone who will pay you to write and report for a few years.

For undergraduate school, I encourage everyone considering journalism to embrace a broad, liberal education. Take some journalism classes if you like and definitely work on school publications or broadcasts as much as possible, but our field badly needs people with broad-based knowledge, not technical training. You can learn about the business as you go, but you won't learn history, psychology, biology, religion, ethics, literature, statistics, or the other things you'll need to see the world as it is and explain it sensibly to your audience.

With all that in mind, here are four basic ideas that can make journalism better, that can help restore the confidence of consumers.

## REINING IN PROMISCUOUS ANONYMITY

My first suggestion is simple and short: The use of anonymous sources in news should be radically curtailed if not very nearly eliminated.

There are certainly times where the only way to tell an important story is through the use of anonymous sources, but their widespread use has become poisonous not only to our credibility but to our ability to tell important stories. The debacle of the "Russiagate" coverage was substantially a product of excessive use of anonymous sources who used the privilege of anonymity to create false narratives and mistaken expectations.

I will not bang on about a topic that many, particularly Jack Shafer, have railed against effectively for years. So I will only add this: Reporters themselves are the ones who should most eagerly embrace this reform, since it is their own credibility that is getting used up by the blind quotes of self-interested sources.

## AVOIDING CATEGORY ERRORS

If we want to have a better conversation about politics, we need a lexicon that reflects reality. When the Associated Press refers to "an ascendant generation of conservatives" who are neutral on Russian aggression, it really means "Republicans" or "right-wingers."[15] When *The New Yorker* calls Fox News knockoff Newsmax a "conservative media company" it's really talking about "pro-Trump" or "nationalist."[16]

When *Politico* writes about "the liberal 'Squad'" in the House that includes members like Rashida Tlaib and Alexandria Ocasio-Cortez, it really means "Democratic Socialist" or "left-wing."[17] When Fox News prime-time favorite Glenn Greenwald says "liberals are obsessed with finding ways to silence and censor their adversaries," he is talking about values that are *illiberal*.[18] It would make no more sense than saying "vegetarians are obsessed with finding ways to eat more beef and pork."

In Greenwald's case, it is pretty obviously tendentious bologna. In the piece referenced above, he uses "liberal" interchangeably with "Democratic" in a category that includes everything from Google to campus protesters. If an ideological group is that capacious, it is useless for anything but fallacious argumentation.

Greenwald's trick is not dissimilar to one used by one of his favorite targets, President Biden. Biden said those members of the Senate, like Kyrsten Sinema, who opposed lowering the chamber's sixty-vote threshold for legislation to jam through a hodgepodge of election legislation were on the same side as Bull Connor and Jefferson Davis. If a category is so broad as to include the rabid segregationist who directed the brutality against civil rights protesters in Birmingham, Alabama, the president of the Confederacy, *and* a forty-five-year-old woman from Arizona who is the first openly bisexual member of the United States Senate, then it is not a category at all, just a smear.

Fortunately, most of the journalistic abuses of political categories are not of Greenwald's kind, but are the result of some combination of ignorance and the rapid evolution in the American political ecosystem in the past fifteen or so years.

The post–World War II political consensus forged between Americans born after the war and the members of their parents' generation relied on a left-right ideological continuum that roughly aligned with the terms "liberal" and "conservative." The horrors of Soviet communism and German fascism had been sufficient to substantially trim off the dangling edges on each side in the second half of the twentieth century.

A "liberal" was someone like Orwell who believed in absolute human rights and individual dignity, but favored generous welfare and tough treatment of the rich and wealthy corporations and who took a dim view of traditional values. A "conservative" was someone like William F. Buckley who favored laissez-faire economics, limited government, and traditional values, but who also staunchly supported individual liberty and defending the natural rights of humankind.

There were those at the left edge, like former vice president Henry Wallace, the Soviet apologist who ran for president in 1948, and those at the right edge, like former Alabama governor George Wallace, no relation, who ran as a right-wing nationalist in 1968. But the mainstream conversation was between people who agreed on *liberty* as an essential virtue. Liberals wanted a more generous welfare state and less restrictive cultural rules. Conservatives wanted smaller government and traditional values. There were lots of exceptions and contradictions, but the liberal/left/Democrat and conservative/right/Republican over-lays mostly worked.

It was, in many ways, a continuation of the debate between members of the Founders' generation. There were those, like Thomas Paine and Thomas Jefferson, who believed that there should be few restrictions to the will of the people on the direction of government authority, and there were those, like Edmund Burke and Alexander Hamilton, who sought more safeguards against mob rule. Despite profound disagreements about the way to balance freedom and order, all would have agreed that every government should derive its authority from the will of the governed and that every person (more complicated in Jefferson's case) had natural or God-given rights that governments were obliged to defend, regardless of popular sentiment.

But the through-line has not always been clear, as we saw in Chapter 1 with the rise of fascistic and dictatorial sentiments among many Americans in the 1930s. At that point, as in other moments throughout our history, the debate has shifted from the foundational American disagreement over how best to balance individual liberty with a government of sufficient authority to meet the demands of the electorate. In these moments, like our own, the debate is not just how to balance the competing aims of the American system of government but whether the American system is adequate to the demands of modern life.

When the *Washington Post* offers a view that "'freedom' was historically and remains intertwined with Whiteness" and the then-op-ed editor for the *New York Post* writes about the need to "fight the culture war with the aim of defeating the enemy and enjoying the spoils," it's clear that even in mainstream spaces, the old consensus around liberty and self-determination is pretty

well shredded.[19] In a time of political transition like our own, the
terms of the previous century, "liberal" and "conservative," are
insufficient.

I believe journalists should, within the bounds of honesty,
call people and their groups and institutions what they want to
be called. We should never do what Greenwald does and intentionally mislabel people to bolster our own arguments. But we
also have to develop a lexicon that relates to real life in order to
hammer out a new consensus. There are ongoing, intense struggles on the left and the right and within the two parties that
broadly represent their interests not only about the value of liberty
and self-determination, but among the subfactions themselves.

Over here is a Democratic Socialist, yonder is a progressive.
Over there is a "national conservative," around the way is a
"common good conservative." For people who are focused on
these kinds of atomic-level differences or the power struggle
within intense minority groups, these are worthwhile labels to
explore. But when we are talking about the new politics of our
era, some broader groupings are necessary.

Here's the lexicon I made for myself:

- **Conservatism** seeks to conserve the vision of the American Founding and the constitutional system developed
  to protect individual's natural rights, broadly identified as
  "life, liberty, and the pursuit of happiness." It sees expan-
  sions of government power, especially at the federal level,
  as inimical to the preservation of individuals' rights under
  the Constitution. The conservative view generally opposes
  social engineering but may favor "nudges" to encourage virtue among America's citizens, and certainly seeks

to undo or block rules or requirements that they believe undermine traditional values.

- **Liberalism** seeks to champion universal principles of liberty, many of which also informed the Founding, but is not limited to those principles or this country. While American conservatism could not be understood as such in much of the West, where that term is more synonymous with "traditionalism," liberalism would sound much the same around the globe. The "four freedoms" described by Franklin Roosevelt—freedom of speech, freedom of worship, freedom from want, freedom from fear—that were the basis for the United Nations Charter provide a good overview of the liberal worldview.

- **Progressivism** seeks to ameliorate the problems of humankind by lifting up the downtrodden, but not necessarily within the framework of the American system or the humanistic concept of natural rights. Progressivism today is different from its version of a century ago in some ways, but the core belief remains: Scientific and technological advances have made it possible to defeat human nature and the ills that have plagued humankind for ten millennia. The emphasis among conservatives and liberals on individuality and self-determination for all prevents necessary steps from being taken to rebalance the injustices of the existing system. The phrase "big, structural change," favored by Senator Elizabeth Warren, describes the kind of transformation progressives seek. So, if free speech is a tool exploited by racists to maintain white supremacy, or private property rights are a means to subjugate the poor, then free speech and private property rights should be curtailed.

Progressives are not liberal in any of the most meaningful senses of the word, except for in expenditures.

- **Nationalism** seeks the betterment of the American nation and its people but not necessarily its founding principles. In this view, the individual rights at the center of the Founders' project have been used against the common good. Nationalists believe that the appropriate aim of the federal government should always be the improvement of life for the greatest number of Americans, even when that comes at a cost to individual rights greater than a strict reading of the Constitution would allow. This is an approach that sees many ideas of the Founding and the Enlightenment from which it flowed as a danger to the American nation itself. The view holds that the nation should be kept safe from perceived dangers external, like immigration and cheap goods from other countries, while the federal power should be used to engineer an economy and a culture more suitable to the Judeo-Christian values they espouse. This is a style of conservatism common around the world but is unlike the traditional American concept.

This is, like any such lexicon, too broad to apply perfectly. Some progressives are more liberal than others. Some conservatives have strong nationalist leanings. But we have to start somewhere. Journalists covering politics need more precise terms to facilitate a more useful discussion. Opinion journalists participating in such a discussion need common language to be understood by news consumers. Whether you use this construction or your own, the debate needs more than the post–World War II idea of left-liberal/right-conservative.

If we say that the nationalists in the Freedom Caucus are conservatives and the members of the Squad are liberal, then we will reinforce the idea that their radical departures from liberalism or conservatism are actually more pure or intense versions of the original.

As we see on matters like using federal authority to break up tech companies and/or regulate speech online, the fundamental disagreements are between progressives and liberals and nationalists and conservatives. The progressives and nationalists agree on *whether* the government has such broad powers, but not on how to impose them. Liberals and conservatives tend to get off at the first stop.

The struggles of the 2020s and 2030s are very often going to make strange bedfellows of nationalists and progressives and conservatives and liberals. We should acknowledge as much with our terms.

## PRESERVING HUMILITY

How powerful is the news media? How powerful are individual media outlets and journalists?

Probably not as powerful as most of us—whether we are consumers or producers of news—tend to think. Americans of all ideological stripes are prone to see the news, whether for good or for ill, as more important than it really is. Not surprisingly, no one is as susceptible to this notion as the members of my own vocation. What could be more flattering than the idea that our coverage and commentary is actually steering the ship of state?

We live in a time when news coverage has never been greater in volume, but the quality of that coverage seems to be constantly in decline. It's a kind of informational inflation in which there is too much news chasing consumers and the value of that news is not what it used to be.

But you wouldn't know that from the way the right-wing critics of the press talk about it. The gang that Donald Trump called "the enemy of the American people" probably couldn't muster being the enemy of all the Albanians, let alone the whole United States. If the news business was the kind of threat that many on the right claim, one would think that we would have come up with a way to actually, you know, make money and not keep going bankrupt.

Nor would you know about this news inflation to listen to left-wingers who talk on and on about "disinformation." To hear them tell it, the members of the American public are clustered around their Marconi sets hanging on every word from every news outlet like they were waiting for a fireside chat. It is certainly true that there are plenty of dupes and suckers out there. Somebody has to go to political rallies, after all. But it seems obvious that the far bigger group is the one that believes almost nothing that is being reported. The folks who want information czars apparently haven't noticed how few Americans care about the news at all.

Grandiosity, though, isn't just the province of those who hate the press. It belongs also to its members. Even as consumption of news declines, journalists remain prone to imagining that our role in shaping elections, government, and cultural trends is unchanged. Part of this may be the fault of the invention of Twitter, a machine that both depletes the value of journalism by dribbling out coverage in an endless gurgle but also enhances reporters' sense of their own importance by creating a large echo chamber into which they can holler affirmations of self-worth.

In Chapter 3, we discussed the *New York Times*' front-page declaration in August 2016 that the time had come to put away dainty ideas about balance in political coverage. The paper put the blame on the Republican presidential nominee: "Trump is testing the norms of objectivity in journalism."[20] It was because of Trump that journalists had to set aside "any one campaign's definition of fairness" to tell a version of events that "will stand up to history's judgment." This thinking, of course, is what helped so many political journalists before and after get down in the mud with Trump and try to fight him as an opposing force.

Trump and his supporters have often equated the misdeeds and lies of the then-president with unfair or dishonest media coverage. I would rebut the claim by pointing out that one of the parties in question was the sitting president and the other was a newspaper or television station. The imbalance in both power and duty was so great as to turn any equivalency nonsensical. But many in the press actually share the view of our industry as an equivalent power.

In Chapter 4 we talked about how our political leaders outsource their responsibilities to the news media so they can focus on celebrities themselves. There are more than a few who believe that they are not only equal to the task, but are appropriate custodians of a totally different kind of power than the American system imagines for the press. When Representative Matt Gaetz wrote that "we are governed by the theater geeks from high school," he revealed his own misunderstands of power.[21] But he also offered a great compliment to any power-hungry theater geeks out there.

The defining struggle in most of our lives, however we earn our livings, is honest self-evaluation. If we can't see ourselves as we are—or close to it—there's no chance we can be the people we were made to be or called to become.

All humans struggle with this, but journalists get to try this high-wire act in front of a larger audience. This is why we tend to be particularly embarrassed about our mistakes and prone to hiding from them.

"Political predictions are usually wrong. But even when one makes a correct one, to discover why one was right can be very illuminating. In general, one is only right when either wish or fear coincides with reality," George Orwell wrote in his 1946 essay "In Front of Your Nose." "If one recognizes this, one cannot, of course, get rid of one's subjective feelings, but one can to some extent insulate them from one's thinking and make predictions cold-bloodedly. . . ."[22]

I can feel Orwell looking over his spectacles at me every time I'm trying to figure out how an election is going to turn out or which bill might succeed or fail. Have I been cold-blooded enough, or did my feelings get in the way? Humility for a political forecaster and analyst is very much about understanding how susceptible we all are to seeing our hopes or fears instead of the way things really are. But other kinds of journalism rely more on other kinds of humility.

In one of his last pieces before leaving his perch as *New York Times* media columnist to launch a new news outlet, Ben Smith interviewed Brandon Brown, the twenty-eight-year-old stock car driver whose first-ever NASCAR win was overshadowed by the chants of "F--k Joe Biden," misheard by the trackside reporter as "Let's go Brandon."[23] It is a very sad story. Here is a seemingly nice, respectful young man whose pinnacle career moment to date has been turned into a dumb vulgarity. Brown is a Republican but wants nothing to do with the taunt against the president. But neither does he want to alienate the overwhelmingly anti-Democrat NASCAR audience.

When Brown agreed to be interviewed by Smith, he was willingly strapping himself in with one of the most unflinching interviewers in the business. The perils would have been just as real with a reporter from Fox News or another "let's go Brandon" kind of outlet, too. But the cultural distance added a layer with Smith. Yale-graduate New Yorkers who are renowned tastemakers are not the obvious go-to for people who hang around with pit crews in Woodbridge, Virginia.

Smith could have given Brown enough rope to hang himself, gently leading the conversation back to hot-button issues until the subject said something that could produce a rage-click headline. Or Smith could have squeezed Brown with gotcha questions. What did he think about the way NASCAR has treated black drivers? Does Brown condone the racism shown by some fans, etc. Smith did neither.

"He seemed resigned to the ritual of being interviewed by a newspaper reporter, and I think would have sat there with me by the track for quite a while more, navigating subjects he's never really thought about," Smith wrote. "We never got that far. It just didn't seem fair. I found myself thinking that I would prefer to live in a country that permits racecar drivers, actors and musicians to avoid being grilled by people like me, and I made a quick exit."[24]

In a recent interview of my own, I asked Smith about the decision to not make Brown another log on the culture war bonfire and if he would have done the same thing in the same situation ten years ago. "Probably not," he allowed.[25]

More of that, please.

## KEEPING POLITICS IN ITS PLACE

I discovered even as a teenager starting out in the news business that everyone must produce some filler to go around all the car ads and legal notifications.

Every newspaper where I ever worked would run special sections or themed coverage on advertiser-preferred topics. The sales department would cook up some idea, and then our bosses in the newsroom would tell us the bad news: In addition to our regular grind, we had to puff up some fluff.

"We're doing a spring garden special section. I need at least one story from everybody on outdoor living." Urp. "We're sponsoring the car show. I need a write-up on the top Toyota dealers." Gurgle. These are trade-offs that I made to pay for my platform. Writing up the new railroad-tie terraced gardens at a senior living center or explaining the sales philosophy of the guy who sold the most Camrys (hint: it's always personal connections) was not afflicting the comfortable, nor comforting the afflicted. But it was a worthwhile trade-off to me for the chance to avoid getting a straight job with quarterly performance reviews and TPS reports. A small price, I figured.

The resulting #journalism may only have been something to appear next to an ad for mulch, but mulch ads helped pay my salary. And if I only had to do it a few times a year, I didn't feel too guilty about it. Plus, some people apparently do love mulching, even if the thought makes me want to jam a garden trowel in my eye.

These special sections would be akin to the sponsored online content you see today, like the Rolex-sponsored climate countdown-to-doom sponsorship at the *Washington Post* or BuzzFeed listicles like "32 Products That'll Make You Think 'Wow, This Is A Need,'" where the publisher gets a cut of the sales.[26] It's icky, but not entirely avoidable when you're starting out, so I just tried to minimize the volume until I was established enough to not have to do sponsored quasi news. I worked on some partnerships while I was at Fox—debate cosponsors, social media tie-ins, etc.—but it's been a long time since I had to do any mulch-forward content.

The best way I found to stay away from cheesy filler dreamed up by others was to produce cheesy filler I got to make up myself.

A newsroom is like a firehouse. You need enough people to do the job when there is a major event, but that means that you will have surplus workers when there is less going on. The same goes for the advertising. Though there have been lots of changes from dynamic advertising rates, news outlets can't just sell the big news days. They're looking for constant revenue. If there isn't enough hard news to fill all the column inches or airtime that the ad department sold, you need something else.

I wish I could tell you that I struggled with how to do that as a reporter; that I had really struggled with my desire to spend long days and nights practicing community journalism to reflect the struggles and passions of the downtrodden. I wish I could tell you that I told the bosses that there would be no fluff, but that every inch of newsprint opposite those ads would be my words championing the oppressed.

I did not choose to make humanity's plight the content of my filler. Not that my bosses would have refused me. Except for a brief stint in local TV news, I have never had any sense that I couldn't write or talk about any topic, as long as it was basically newsworthy or interesting. And I have certainly done advocacy journalism, including some that I am proud of. But in the space between big stories or in lulls on a beat, I just don't have it in me to go be Upton Sinclair. It seemed boring and kind of pompous to me. What I did do long ago was determine that both the readers and I would enjoy whatever filler I produced. Or at least I would . . .

I filed stories from every corner of the state of West Virginia. I wrote up buckwheat festivals and white-water rafting trips, a ski slope reunion for Vietnam vets, golf course reviews, and spent the day with Snake Girl and the carnival freak show. I did human interest stories that would make my eyes well up. I met characters that Thomas Wolfe or Eudora Welty couldn't have dreamed up. I have turned in expense reports for a Giovanni sandwich-eating contest, breakfast in a topless bar, cab fare for a drunken paranormal investigator, 20-gauge shotgun shells, hotel rooms for a stranded Japanese TV crew, and a blue blazer that was burned by an experimental jet engine. Not all for one story, mind you . . .

I maintain my policy to this day. I say, if it's going to be filler, let it be some combination of wholesome, delightful, uplifting, silly, or just plain weird. Some of the best stories I have ever done or seen came from the little spaces in between what's "important." If a reporter or an outlet is doing the rest of the job right, there's more than enough that is serious, depressing, and dry. In the news business you call them "brights," those little pieces that illuminate the gloom of serious coverage a bit.

That's why my political newsletters always include at least one funny story and one story totally apart from politics: history, science, music, food, etc. If you expect someone to make it through three thousand words about campaign finance reports, polls, and the gaseous pronouncements of politicians, you have to let them exhale along the way.

I told you that story so I could tell you this one: West Virginia had one potato chip maker, Mister Bee. When I had been a reporter in Charleston for a few years and had figured out my penchant for fun fluff, Mister Bee went through some kind of big expansion or ownership change and was in the news. If you are not from a small state, this will sound very strange, but in West Virginia, anything that is uniquely our own must be intently examined. Ask any West Virginian about Fiestaware, the colorful ceramic dishes, and you will likely get a full report about Homer Laughlin China and the world's largest teapot in Chester, West Virginia. So, yes, a potato chip company can be a matter of news interest.

So, espying an opportunity to keep my story count up for the week when the courthouse was slow—as well as a chance to have some fun—I pitched a potato chip taste test: blind tastings by the newsroom staff, lots of groany puns, mock seriousness masking actual intensity of the participants, etc. Well, Mister Bee was more like Mister Eff in the rankings. The company has changed hands at least once I know of in the intervening twenty years, so this is no reflection of its current offerings, but compared to national and regional brands back then, Mister Bee did not make the cut. I wrote up my little story and didn't think any more of it. Until I heard from the then owner, who was *livid*. He told me how he had let another reporter have access to his plant for an unrelated story and how he assumed that we would be treating him favorably.

I was so young that it had never really occurred to me that people regularly assumed those kinds of quid pro quos were part of coverage. But this dude was furious that we panned his chips—chips for which he had been on a publicity blitz. It would be better for him, his workers, his community, and the state if we all just said good things about his product.

It's funny to think of today, but I was *so* offended. How dare he think that I, intrepid reporter, would rig a taste test? That I would sell out over chips? Calumny!

That was a big moment in my education. Most of the people who find themselves dealing with the press are there to either get something publicized or prevent something from being publicized. It perhaps sounds like an obvious point to nonjournalists, but the long-standing, deep mistrust of our business is in part rooted in those expectations.

The man from Mister Bee was wrong to think that he should have automatically gotten a favorable review even if his chips were greasy and flat-tasting. But he was not wrong about everything. I should have considered the costs to him and his employees not as we were judging or I was writing, but when I first conceived of the story. For me, it was a fun way to kill an afternoon on a slow news day and eat potato chips with my friends. For my newspaper, it was a cute story to run on the front of the lifestyle section on some random weekday. For people trundling spuds in a Wood County potato chip plant, it was about something more significant.

I shouldn't have been flippant or felt so entitled. They deserved better than to have some reporter do a drive-by that left them looking bad. It's not that I should have lied and said they were delicious, and if I were a food writer or worked at some snack food industry publication it would have been wholly appropriate to have panned Mister Bee. But not as filler. I think about those greasy chips with some regularity as I consider appropriate topics for my commentary and analysis or when directing the coverage of others.

The best filler is that which doesn't feel like filler.

Imagine an x-axis running from hard news at one end—the kind we call "commodity news." It's the announcement of the landing of the Mars rover, the Russian tanks crossing the frontier, the results of the Senate vote: factual events that are almost universally available and reported simultaneously. This is the core function of the Associated Press. As we move up the scale, we come to investigative reporting. These are hard news, fact-based stories that are the product of a single news organization. This is the first place filler can show up.

Most local TV news broadcasts set their advertising rates based on the results of quarterly "sweeps" by Nielsen. If you live in one of the top twenty-five markets—New York to Portland, Oregon—your local TV viewership is measured much the same way as Nielsen does its national numbers: A select number of households are outfitted with meters that electronically monitor and report to the ratings company what was being watched and when. Like a political survey, this data is extrapolated to the market or the nation as a whole.[27]

For the next thirty-one largest markets—Baltimore to Wilkes-Barre, Pennsylvania—there are still some meters, but because of smaller market size and revenue, Nielsen also relies on diaries filled out by members of households selected quarterly for a small payment and the thrill of getting to impose their viewing habits on others.[28] But for markets 57 (Little Rock, Arkansas) through 210 (Glendive, Montana) local ratings are based entirely by diary collection in "sweeps" months: February, May, July, and November.

This is why your local news looks like *Dateline NBC* every third month. "Could what you don't know about your child's crib be deadly? Tonight at eleven, you'll find out. News Team 4, on your side . . ." Or elder scams or elevated arsenic levels or a dry cleaner that lost some wedding dresses. Every time I see these spots, I think how strange it sounds that a TV station would know how to save the lives of babies or the elderly, but they're not going to tell you until *after* you watch *NCIS: Hawaii*. But of course, they don't know, so they're not really holding out. What they usually do have is a government watchdog agency or a plaintiffs' lawyer that has a case against said crib maker, telemarketer, nursing home, water treatment plant, dry cleaner, etc. Going it alone would expose the TV station to lawsuits, so it's safer to follow someone else's lead.

Target selection is important here. I developed an obsession about the crummy video gambling parlors the state of West Virginia licensed to pick the pockets of poor people in order to shield lawmakers from their jobs of either cutting spending or raising taxes. But those machines were not just important to politicians; they were big business for the companies that provided the machines. And, not surprisingly, those companies had powerful political connections.[29] This made lots of people uncomfortable, and my story suggestions were often unpopular with management. But if you can find some mom-and-pop store somewhere that's breaking food storage rules or some benighted government office that is always failing at its task, you've got a sweeps package for sure.

The way Nielsen measures local news ratings encourages quarterly investigative journalism—or at least sensationalistic advertising of it, but the local market and political pressures and limited newsroom budgets encourage fluffy investigations. So, moving just one step away from hard "commodity" news has already opened the door for filler. As soon as you bring in self-selection by news outlets, filler will soon follow. Courageous investigative journalism is critically important and in pitifully short supply. Part of the reason is that very often filler is passed off as the real thing, diminishing the value of investigations themselves.

At the far end of the x-axis is content that is transparently intended as filler: sponsored sections, marketing tie-ins, celebrity gossip, etc. These are not things that any news consumer needs, but some may want it. This is the obvious junk, and, accordingly, I don't worry about it. No thinking person believes they're consuming real news when they gobble up paparazzi pictures, BuzzFeed listicles, or the gushy segment about whichever celebrity's plant-based, age-defying lifestyle brand.

Nor do I worry about actual lifestyle or culture coverage. It is not strictly *necessary* but it certainly adds value for consumers if done well. A news outlet's civic responsibility certainly extends to the culture. There's not only no shame in the dining-out section or the movie reviews, or back-to-school shopping guides or the updates on the value of antioxidants or goat yoga. Especially on the local level, this is the kind of filler that helps to keep a community strong. Like anything, it can be done wrong: sensationalized, biased, with a hidden economic agenda, etc. But fluff for fluff's sake is fine by me as a concept.

It's the stuff that runs all the way from the faux investigatory sweeps package to celebrity news disguised as issue coverage that causes the trouble. When you tell people that the wall-to-wall reporting of Britney Spears's court-ordered conservatorship is about mental health or about a debate over involuntary commitments, you are allowing them to believe that something that is not news but is really lurid and maybe even prurient is actually wholesome. Under the guise of wellness and lifestyle coverage, the news business has found awful ways to emotionally manipulate consumers and pass off trash as the real thing. This is where consumers are made to worry, envy, judge, and resent for profit.

We like to imagine that the assault on self-esteem began with social media, but it's been no secret for a century that emotional manipulation through ghoulish "lifestyle" coverage is big business. Except for my strong penchant for sharing recipes and methods for cooking delicious meats, and the little diversions I always include in my political newsletters, I have always kept myself safe from this end of the axis.

The kind of filler that is my lot to sift and sort makes up a great deal of the continuum between fluff for fluff's sake and hard news at the other end. Politics, even when I started in the business, was a "sometimes" thing. Political reporters were also typically government reporters, following the politicians from incumbency to candidacy and then back again. The campaign season started to warm up in the late winter of every even-numbered year as primary season began, but would move to the back burner through the spring and summer. By Labor Day it was time to get it going in a big way for the final seven- or eight-week stretch to Election Day. Outside of those windows, I had to find honest work covering the winners of the elections or something else entirely. That calendar still roughly holds for *campaign* coverage, but *political* coverage is now eternal.

If you cover government at any level, this is supposed to be substantially different than purely political coverage. Covering the government is reporting on what people in power are doing, want to do, or have been prevented from doing. Political coverage is reporting, or often analysis, of how events will affect future elections. Government coverage: "Bill advances with bipartisan support." Political coverage: "Bipartisan win for president deals blow to primary challengers' hopes." But if you've read this far, you already know how often those things get tangled up.

Some intertwining is inevitable. Most politicians in office want to stay in power more than almost anything else. As they make their calculations about what to do or not to do, they're thinking about how it will improve their chances of keeping their current position or moving up. But what has happened over time is that my specialty—politics and elections—has crowded out government coverage to such a degree that we're losing our capacity to produce it or consume it.

Almost anything can be made into political coverage because nearly every controversy or topic can be found to potentially have political ramifications, especially to a partisan audience. Hence the scramble to politicize COVID-19. If it was just a shared crisis with no clear solution, that's depressing and disorienting. But if it can be made into a red problem or a blue problem, people can stay tuned confident that they are on the right side.

When a Muslim man killed scores at a gay nightclub in Orlando, Florida, in June 2016, it was one of the rare times where all sides could play the story to the hilt. Had the suspected killer been a right-wing extremist like the ones charged with attacking the Tree of Life congregation in Pittsburgh or the Emanuel African Methodist Episcopal Church in Charleston, South Carolina, Republican-leaning viewers would have soon tired of the coverage of an angry white man slaughtering minorities. That's a left-wing narrative about racist gun nuts and therefore perceived as bad for Republicans. If the victims had been white Christians at church or members of the military or police, many Democratic viewers would have soon wearied of what they would have perceived as a right-wing narrative about jihadists run amok and therefore bad for Democrats.

If political ramifications are the primary focus of coverage, it guarantees that dealing with the actual issue itself becomes harder. We very often don't talk about border security, but rather the *politics* of border security. We don't cover what was in the bill; we cover the *politics* of the bill. Even pandemics and war get fed into the politicization machine. Politicians are the ones mostly doing it, but they are doing it with journalists as the intended initial audience. And we are suckers for it. Politics means conflict, hot words, personalities, and lots of leeway for analysis and subjectivity. Government means boring, specific policies.

To make politics interesting to the broadest possible audience, it must be made to appear important when very often it is not. This hype is nothing new. But what is relatively new is the possibility to have it produce large, highly habituated audiences. As we've seen throughout the book, politics has particular power to attract and maintain news consumers even after the demise of the industry's old business model. Outlets are therefore looking for whatever they can find to ensorcell the users who came for the politics. Outlets are not going to offer them something different; they're going to give them more of the same. That means making lots of new "political junkies" to follow every bit of lip-flap and consequence-free tweet as if they were meaningful. Politics is treated as something appropriate to obsess about, even when it has become disconnected for policy or electoral consequences.

Doing this about the wild-card playoff game or dream motor homes or science fiction shows or professional cornhole championships or military history or fudge brownies is fine. Some people become obsessed with inanities. Their priorities may get so out of whack that they take an unhealthy interest in things that are not essential. If you have time enough to be an obsessive about anything that doesn't feed, clothe, delight, protect, encourage, educate, or otherwise love your fellow man, you might have achieved a level of financial success that allows you to have both wholesome and indulgent obsessions. If you have, congratulations. But I think many of us can have only two passions—often familial and professional—while still more of us have only one passion, often unhealthy in nature. Another legion of luckless souls has no passion at all.

But the dangers of excessive passion don't mean you shouldn't kick back and take in the televised cornhole championship—the only sports championship to my knowledge that is sponsored by a baked bean company. One of the most amazing broadcasting talents of all is the capacity of a Jack Buck or a Keith Jackson to bring listeners along for a thrilling ride. I one time heard Jackson call an America's Cup race for ABC's *Wide World of Sports*. He may not have known a jib from a jibe any more than I, but he managed to make a boat race as compelling as a college football third-and-long.

Bantery bloviation is fine when it discusses matters of little importance. When it comes to news, though, making things compelling comes at a different cost, especially to its obsessives and our country. Turning politics into filler is not only unworthy, it is dangerous.

As I wandered through the dispersing crowd outside the Capitol on the late afternoon of January 6, 2021, I was struck by how the people I was passing reminded me of fans after a sporting event. There were team colors and some people had coolers and camp chairs as they were trudging back to their cars. These were not the people who had smashed windows and bludgeoned police officers that day. These were folks who had come for then-president Trump's rally and to see the show, maybe to apply some pressure on what they were deceived to believe was an opportunity to shape the outcome of the election. Despite the tear gas hanging in the air, they were obviously still unaware of the shameful, tragic events that unfolded inside the building. One little group even asked to take a selfie with me. It was not the tear gas making my eyes water when I told them why it was not a day for frivolity.

The percentage of news coverage that is either explicitly or implicitly political is so unhealthful in large part because it creates a false impression that politics itself is a worthwhile passion. Take it from a man who has devoted his professional life to politics and elections: It is not.

I love my work and I am passionate about it. I get genuinely excited about poll data and demographics. I have a disturbingly

deep knowledge of political history and arcana. This is part—
though only part—of what makes me a weird person. This was
ordained long ago, and if it weren't politics and history, I suppose
it would have been something else that I never tired of thinking
about, writing about, and talking about. Let's say that I felt the
way I do about forecasting politics about forecasting the weather,
and I had become a meteorologist instead of a political analyst.
That might be a suitable professional passion for me, but it would
not make the weather a worthwhile mainstay for news coverage
at the outlets where I worked. Just because I was tweaking on
nimbostratus patterns and derechos would not make the weather
a worthy subject for around-the-clock coverage.

Local news and, of course, the Weather Channel do their
best to make weather into a big deal every day. There are obviously people who become attached to weather coverage in
unhealthy ways. Fortunately, their obsessions can't actually
change the weather. In politics, though, cultivating anxious
addicts—"junkies"—changes the process. If *Politico*, which was
intended as a specialty publication for people who work in and
around politics, was worth $1 billion to its new owners, some-
thing is way out of whack.[30]

Every news outlet has to fill up all those minutes or all those
inches. Politics is perhaps the easiest way to fill them up in a way
that will produce the strongest connection with consumers. But
all this political filler is killing us.

We live in a republic in which citizens delegate their authority to elected representatives at the local, state, and national level.
We hold elections every two years in which Americans are able
to keep the elected leaders they have or replace them. In between,
there's just not that much to do if you're not actually in politics
and government.

Instead, the news business treats politics like sports, and that leads consumers to believe that if they wear the team colors and root harder, it will change the outcome of the game. Alas, it does, just not in the way that the superfans hope. The constant attention on politics instead of government—on gaining power instead of its exercise—makes the players on the field want to show off to the fans in the stands, instead of trying to win the game. This is partly how you get a country in which a shrinking number of people are civically engaged, but their engagement occurs at unhealthy levels. If politics is mostly pointless fan service with little connection to policy changes, who needs it?

So choose your filler wisely, and see what I failed to see in a bag of greasy chips. Even the fluff has consequences.

# 7.

---

# AN INSIDE JOB

## How to Live a Better Life and Make a Better Country through News Judgment

*In proportion as the structure of a government gives force to public opinion, it is essential that public opinion should be enlightened.*

—George Washington, Farewell Address, 1796

Behold our man, middle-aged and built like a small can of biscuits. He's lightly pacing outside the men's room in the gleaming corridor of the new $391.5 million, fourteen-gate concourse at Ronald Reagan Washington National Airport.[1]

The first thing you apprehend is just as he intended: an olive green, graphic T-shirt prominently featuring a giant, swirly pile of feces buzzing with flies. Beneath it in bold, block type is the word "HAPPENS." Ha. Ha. Ha. He is wearing oversized cargo shorts and his coronavirus mask is pulled down for the sake of a discreetly animated phone call—just enough to reveal a little Fu Manchu mustache riding his upper lip like a freshly waxed boogie board.

Our man clearly has a message for you. He wants you to know he is 1) a dumbass and 2) cool with that.

If you saw him pacing outside of, say, a Long John Silver's in Chillicothe, Ohio, or a vape shop in Tempe, Arizona, you would find our man unremarkable. He would, at first blush, seem very much to belong to the group of people Charles Murray described in his 2012 book, *Coming Apart*, as being from "Fishtown"—part of the 80 percent of white Americans who are falling ever further away from success and social order.[2]

But our man is surrounded by swiftly striving residents of Murray's "Belmont"—the ever more educated, ever more elitist 20 percent—in their severely business-casual, slope-shouldered blazers or three-hundred-dollar yoga pants. It is indeed possible to wear only breathable, moisture-wicking, stretchy fabric from head to toe and still look totally uptight. So what exactly is our man doing here with these people on a briskly commercial Tuesday morning?

Look closer. What's that peeking out of his adult backpack? The handle of a racquetball racquet. What's on that cap clipped to his bag? Titleist. Our man not only has means enough to fly through an expensive airport at a busy time, but is also a serious devotee of two clubby sports. I would not try to carry an extra pack of chewing gum through America's dehumanizing, arbitrarily policed air travel system. This fortysomething man in a shirt with a huge pile of excrement on it will pay the price for maximum touch and feel in his travel racquetball game.

How do we explain the means and opportunity of our friend, given his enthusiasm for looking like he's selling marijuana edibles in the parking lot of a Widespread Panic concert? Maybe he's a trustafarian, frittering away the labors of his ancestors by traveling around to play in regional forty-plus racquetball tournaments? Maybe he got rich quick on the invention of a new flange for pool filters and is flying back from his vacation home after a long weekend. Maybe he has a good job in a laid-back field—PGA caddy, logistics for the band, laser-light show rigger, personal chef, etc. Maybe he has a straight job but is so gifted at it that he can insist on this attire.

Whatever got him here and is taking him somewhere else, it must require the news, right? Even if it's just the weather, our man needs the frickin' info to get where he's going. He's probably not as crass and uncaring as his shirt tells us to believe he is. But even if he were, he would still be interested in sports and sports gambling news. What is Tom Brady up to *now*, he must wonder. Even a blissfully unplugged man-child would need or want some basic information about the world beyond his gaze? Right?

Maybe not.

In a survey last year, pollster Ipsos found that when it came to following "what's going on in politics," 15 percent of American adults identified themselves as following politics "hardly at all."[3] Remember that people do tend to make themselves look better to pollsters, so these are folks who passed up the more respectable-sounding option of "now and then." It wouldn't be unreasonable to believe that there were some additional "hardly at alls" who were passing themselves off as "now and thens."

Anyway, given the saturation of political coverage in most news outlets, you'd have to be pretty checked out of news in general to avoid politics. So while the 15 percent number is an imperfect way to quantify the percentage of ultra-low news consumers in America, it's not a bad jumping-off point.

This certainly could be our man. The group is 60 percent white, 40 percent have at least some college education, and its members are almost exactly evenly distributed among

Republicans, Democrats, and independents. That sounds like a group that could include a raunchy, racquetball-playing jet-setter. The only place where it misses, though, is that ranks of the very checked out are 66 percent female. But who knows? Maybe the turd shirt also comes in contoured, scoop-necked pink and he was on the phone with his wife, who at that very moment was hurtling down the George Washington Parkway in a giant Lexus land yacht to retrieve him?

The opposite is also quite possibly true. He may be a voracious consumer of news and newslike products. His Facebook feed may endlessly bombard his friends and family with witticisms like the one he is offering his fellow travelers on this bright morning. He may be the vanguard of idiocracy, a meme warrior, and a member of the First Mounted Tweet Cavalry. He may consume news-ish content all day.

Television consumption is down from its all-time peak in 2009–10, when the average American household was ingesting almost nine hours of the boob tube every day.[4] Cord cutting rapidly accelerated in the middle of the 2010s, but during the pandemic, cable news usage still reached all-time highs.[5] Plus, the share of Americans getting their news from social media has skyrocketed. In 2021, 48 percent of adults said they turned to social media for news "sometimes" or "often."[6] Taken together, many Americans are now consuming even more than ever, even as the share of news dropouts rises. Not only is *more* news beyond already high levels probably not a good thing; many of us are struggling to sort out this endless wellspring of blather.

According to a December 2020 Pew Research Center report, only 55 percent of adults were "at least fairly confident" that they could discern the difference between news outlets that do their own reporting and those that are just repackaging the work of others.[7] Only 9 percent said they were "very confident." Only 51 percent were aware that Facebook doesn't do its own reporting.

Yeesh.

That's the future of post-journalism America: a country divided between addicted, hyperpartisan super-users who derive a false sense of community and meaning from their connection to the provider on one side, and on the other side, dropouts who understandably avoid the news but in the process become increasingly tuned out of civic life. That means not only that they will not have a government that represents them, but also that they won't have the confidence, skill, or knowledge to do so if they ever do grow up.

On one side, the ill-informed. On the other side, the uninformed.

So what are you going to do about it? In the previous chapter we looked at ways that my fellow journalists and I could be better custodians of the public trust. Now it's your turn.

I have three questions for you to consider as you think about how, how much, and what kind of news you should be consuming. Just as it is the duty of journalists to do our work with the health of the republic and our civil society in mind, you have to consider those things as you consume our product. Plus, you've got your own well-being and happiness to think of.

Many families, including my own, have experienced difficulties around the news in this era of partisan-soaked, around-the-clock consumption.

As my own beloved father approached his eightieth birthday, he purchased a second, *giant* television set for the small sitting area next to his bedroom. He had grown frustrated with not being able to see both Fox News and Fox Business at the same time in full size. Picture-in-picture was not going to feed the bulldog in this situation. When he had both of those suckers on, the radiation from the screens felt like the solar wind in your face.

In the closing years of his life, he and I lost one of our shared loves: talking about politics. He had always been in my lifetime a serious, thoughtful conservative: a former Goldwater volunteer, Reagan devotee, *National Review* subscriber for decades, and someone deeply committed to his Christian faith. I have known few people who lived out the principles of all those beliefs better than John Stirewalt. He loved his neighbor as himself and hated big government all at once, and did both with a smiling serenity.

Much of the change in him was the crabbiness and worry that come to the corners of our minds in old age; the kooky email threads from his work friends didn't help. But my dad—Beez, as I called him—was different in the era of the two televisions. His anger at Barack Obama in 2012 was so intense that in that last year of his life, when I was deeply engaged in the presidential contest and frequently appearing on those screens, I knew to avoid the subject.

It's not that all of what was in that double-barreled blast of content was bad unto itself in those days; it's just that twenty-four hours is not the correct increment in which to consume news— or forty-eight hours, in his case. We were as close as ever when he died; old stories told, favorite poems shared, the finest hymns lifted up. But habitual news consumption had taken something from us.

Our story is far from unique, and far from the worst I've heard. I know of loving families torn apart over pointless, media-driven political controversies. I have friends who no longer speak to one or more parents because their addiction to rage-based coverage, whether left or right, prevents them from being able to have normal conversations anymore. I know grandparents who have never met their grandchildren because of the strife-for-profit business model. I know people who don't go on family vacations to beloved beach houses because they can't stand the sound of cable news blaring at 105 decibels all day and all night.

This is a tragedy, and an avoidable one.

First, don't argue politics with anyone, especially anyone you love. It's pointless. Argument deepens convictions rather than loosening them.

Second, improve your own media habits. Not only will it make you a better citizen; it may help you to see the world through the eyes of others and give you the gift of greater compassion.

Now, on to our three questions.

## ARE YOU INOCULATED AGAINST ARIZONA SYNDROME?

*Check your backpack . . .*

I had a ritual before presidential debates when I worked at Fox. After the audience had all gone through security and made it to their seats, I would take a final walk through the hall to gauge the energy in the crowd.

What had been a matter of curiosity in 2012 became a more important consideration in 2016. Audiences who came to see the candidates savaging one another in gladiatorial combat were getting *rowdy*. Not only were there more blue-collar, Harley-loving folks showing up, but the usually staid members of local Chambers of Commerce and state GOP stalwarts were getting riled. They were interrupting the debates, interfering with camera shots, and cheering and booing with pro-wrestling-level intensity—including at our moderators.

By the time we got to our team's final debate, on March 3 at the fabulous Fox Theatre in Detroit, the energy in the hall was boiling over. I was sincerely worried about the level of hostility toward our on-air crew, Bret Baier, Megyn Kelly, and Chris

Wallace. The race was at a tipping point as conservatives and moderates were making a late effort to block Donald Trump's nomination. Trump had scored well in the Super Tuesday contests but had not put enough daylight between himself and Ted Cruz. Marco Rubio had fizzled but, like John Kasich, was determined to hang around. The Michigan contest five days after the debate between the four remaining candidates was shaping up to be of real significance.

The sprint since the kickoff a month before in Iowa and New Hampshire had been grueling not just because of the work-load, but because I had encountered so much personal hostility from Trump and his supporters. The anger over my analysis and for my role in helping our team develop the toughest questions possible had manifested itself in some occasionally disturbing ways. It was far less than what Megyn and the other anchors were getting, but enough to make me occasionally worry about some nut hurting my sons. Highly unlikely, but nonzero is still an unacceptably high level of risk for some things. So when I walked through the theater, I was expecting the worst.

As I walked up the aisle on stage left, a couple of kindly-looking grannies waved me down. They were just as sweet as they could be and had eager, interested questions. But when I looked down into the backpack at their feet, I saw something shiny. It wasn't anything dangerous. Their open bag was loaded to the top with cans of Icehouse beer. Maybe security let them slide, or just didn't give them close scrutiny. The most exciting thing it looked like they'd be carrying was a needlepoint sampler. Either way, they were there loaded up like it was a tailgate at a Michigan State game.

When one of the women saw that I had seen her stash, she was kind enough to offer me a cold one. I laughed and politely declined, and went to finish my rounds. In that moment, I realized the disconnect between my experience with the race—the experiences of my colleagues, the candidates, the members of their campaigns, and the rest of the media covering the race—and the experience of the electorate. On our side, we were all fighting about serious questions about populism, decorum, the office of the presidency, hate as a political language, Jeb Bush's hoodie . . . But the voters were experiencing it all as *fans*. No wonder: The media and the candidates had made it into some hybrid of sports and reality television. Why wouldn't these old gals treat it as such? Crack a cold one and enjoy the show.

The one thing that truly separates news from entertainment is that sometimes in the news business we have to tell people what they don't want to hear. But that runs smack into the problem that Andrey Miroshnichenko talks about in his theory of post-journalism. If you're trying to maintain your connection with an audience on an emotional level, telling them news that's bad for their side breaks the spell. The outlet isn't just an impartial entity delivering some unpleasant information; it has violated the trust of its highly habituated users.

When I went on-air in 2020 to defend the Decision Desk's call that Joe Biden would win Arizona, I was supremely confident. The team that Arnon Mishkin—whom that year we dubbed "Q-Arnon"—had built was the best in the business. And we had better survey data than the competition, thanks to our partnership with the Associated Press and the National Opinion Research Center. The irony for Fox was that the call that so infuriated Trump and so many viewers was possible only because Rupert Murdoch had four years earlier yanked Fox out of the consortium of other networks paying for exit polls. He sure wasn't wrong. The exit polls were bad and getting worse.

So Arnon & Company built a better mousetrap, and that was even before we found out that the coronavirus pandemic would increase the share of mail-in ballots by as much as 50 percent. You can't do an exit poll if nobody is exiting the polls, so while our competitors were scrambling to put together a system to accommodate the change, we had already tested our superior product in the 2018 midterms. It turned out to be a capability that the network would regret developing.

The rage directed at me was so intense because so many Fox viewers had grown accustomed to the casual exaggerations and relentless happy talk from opinion shows from morning till midnight. Had viewers been given a more accurate understanding of the race over time, Trump's loss would have been seen as a likely outcome. Instead of understanding his narrow win in 2016 as the shocking upset that it was, viewers were told to assume that polls don't apply (unless they were good for Trump) and that forecasters like me were going to be wrong again. But that overlooked the differences in the race from four years earlier. Trump outperformed expectations again, but he was too far down for even a 2016-sized bump to take him to victory.

Amid the geyser of anger in the wake of the Arizona call, Senator Kevin Cramer, Republican of North Dakota, called for my firing and accused me of a "cover-up."[8] Covering up what, exactly? We didn't have any ballots to count and we didn't have any electoral votes to award. We were just some guys with a cool computer, lots of polling data, and a lot of nicotine gum and coffee. But if you've been living comfortably in the climate-controlled emotions of post-journalism, when the real thing comes along, it's a shock to the system.

If you are consuming free news, you are not the customer, you are the product. Free outlets want to capture your attention and keep it as long as possible. Therefore, they have intense incentives to do whatever it takes to keep you glued. This was less of a problem in the old days of consolidated broadcast media, when news outlets had to aim for big, broad audiences. The product wasn't always great, but balance, or at least its appearance, was essential if you wanted to talk to a third of the country. But as we've seen, the partisan concentrations in the audiences for major outlets are so high that broad appeal would be financial suicide today.

That's why you've got to pay for at least some of your news. There are certainly problems with audiences capturing outlets in the fee-based model, but at the very least, it gives an advantage to outlets that want to go for quality over quantity. It doesn't matter how long someone spends with one of my articles at *The Dispatch*, or how many social media interactions it generates. Their subscription rate remains the same, and I don't feel any subtle pressure to sensationalize or whip up false controversy for just a minute or two longer than I should.

I would encourage everyone who can afford it to support at least one national outlet, and one local outlet with their subscription dollars. I do not like every story yielded by my subscriptions to the *Wall Street Journal*, *New York Times*, and, yes, *Washington Post*. But that's okay. In my mind, I'm only paying for the ones I like.

Read, listen, and watch widely. Hear other perspectives than your own. Try on other points of view regularly. If you're conservative, put on NPR in the morning. If you're liberal, try *The Dispatch* (obviously) or seek out opinion pieces from writers like George Will, Ross Douthat, and Peggy Noonan on your editorial page. You will learn a lot, and understand more about where your fellow Americans are coming from. Stick to high-quality sources, but be daring. It won't hurt you to be exposed to other ideas.

Also, it will inoculate you against the kind of bubbled thinking that made the very predictable outcome of 2020's election into a constitutional crisis and a riot at the Capitol. The people who were duped by Trump and his Stop the Steal posse wouldn't have been such easy marks if they had had a varied news diet.

## IS THE CONTROVERSY CONSEQUENTIAL?

*Beware the newsloaf.*

Where there's no conflict, there's little chance you'll find hard news.

When the vote is unanimous, the project is completed on schedule, and the planes all arrive on time, it's not big news. When the Senate deadlocks, the budget is busted, and the airports are socked in by a storm, it's a story.

That's a little grim, I know. But while it is certainly true that good news can be news, too, the most important stories usually involve some tension. Consider what has long been said to be the worst newspaper headline of all time, just three words atop a column in the April 10, 1986, *New York Times*: "Worthwhile Canadian Initiative."[9] No verb, and each word seemingly hand-picked to create an enveloping fog of blandness. It's like an Anne Murray song, but as a headline.

It's helpful for readers when news outlets not only identify the controversy or conflict around an important issue, but also point the disagreement out in clear terms. This can be done in a way that is substantive, not sensational, and, as such, is a hallmark of good journalism.

But that doesn't mean that every controversy is newsworthy.

Media monitoring firm NewsWhip tracked the social media interactions for news stories about twenty-three well-known politicians from January 2021 to January 2022 to see which figures generated the most action online.[10]

At the top of the list were Senator Ted Cruz of Texas and Representative Alexandria Ocasio-Cortez of New York. Close behind were Representatives Marjorie Taylor Greene of Georgia and Rashida Tlaib of Michigan. At the bottom of the rankings were Senate Majority Leader Chuck Schumer, President Biden, Senate Minority Leader Mitch McConnell, and Senators Joe Manchin of West Virginia and Kyrsten Sinema of Arizona.

You see what happened. Four members of Congress who all have notably undistinguished careers as lawmakers generated the most engagement, while the president and the most influential members of the Senate came up as cold as the beers in the bottom of the backpack.

And it's not like the clicks for the ineffectual legislators were a sign of their popularity. Nine of the ten biggest social media stories about Ocasio-Cortez were from right-wing outlets, with almost exactly the same being true in reverse for Greene. But those hate clicks generate money for the outlets, and greater celebrity and fundraising potential for the lawmakers, no matter how little they accomplish.

But the cycle isn't done yet. News outlets routinely do stories about what people are saying about *other* stories. "Twitter blows up . . ." etc. Think of that. Stories about false controversies involving practically irrelevant political figures drive lots of social media engagement for news outlets. Then the news outlet scrapes up the trimmings from Twitter, mashes them together, and sells them again. By now, a story that wasn't even useful for anything but phony outrage has been pulped and reassembled.

You know when you went to the cafeteria and they said they had turkey, but it was really "turkey loaf," a gelatinous log of gobbler bits pressed together and cooked in a steam kettle? Well, this is newsloaf.

A good way to tell the difference between news and newsloaf is to ask this question: Does the story impart new information or does it provide information about people's feelings? A possible follow-up: Are the people in question famous? If you're hearing about famous people talking about their feelings, a hot slab of newsloaf is probably what's for dinner.

If the headline is "Secretary reveals [significant new information] during hearing," you may be in line for the real thing. If it's "Senator goes OFF on cabinet secretary," it's newsloaf all the way, my friend.

We talked in the previous chapter about the dangers of politics as filler, but performative emotional reactions to false controversies regurgitated as stories about Twitter may be the lowest form of that already rock-bottom category.

Almost every news story deals with a controversy. Before you spend any of your precious time on one, ask yourself whether the subject of the controversy makes any difference. If it's really about what people said or how they felt, skip it.

## ARE YOU BEING SKEPTICAL OR CYNICAL?
*"Reason is . . . the slave of the passions."*

One of my bugaboos in the news business are stories about studies like this one: "Smokers have harder time getting jobs, study finds."[11]

That's good enough for some self-satisfied clicks from nonsmokers, passive-aggressive link sharing to smokers, and even some anxiety clicks from those who can't kick the habit. But it's probably bunkum.

The reason that people who smoke have a harder time finding work isn't the smoking, it's the smokers. It's not like risk-averse, squeaky-clean squares with Harvard MBAs and a passion for punctuality get spotted with a pack of Kools sticking out of their fanny packs and get nixed from the hiring list. It's probably that people who smoke are more likely to engage in other risky behaviors and have other disadvantages.

The highest incidence of cigarette smoking among all ethnic groups is American Indians and Alaska Natives (20.9 percent); among all educational levels, it's adults with only a GED certificate (35.3 percent); and among all income levels, it's adults with an annual household income less than $35,000 (21.4 percent).[12] I can't say for sure, but I bet if you did a study and looked at the employment records of members of those disadvantaged groups who *didn't* smoke, you'd probably find substantial lag compared to the population as a whole.

I'd be willing to believe that there might be a difference in employment rates between smokers and nonsmokers *within* each subset, but that's way down the line from "Smokers have harder time getting jobs." That's certainly nothing you could come close to showing in a study that "surveyed 131 unemployed smokers and 120 unemployed nonsmokers." That's capital-B Bunkum right there.

But people love these kinds of stories. Why? Because they confirm their existing biases. If you're a former smoker, it feels very good to hear that your employment prospects are better. If you're a current smoker trying to quit, the same headline triggers concern and, the outlet hopes, a click.

Now, think back to our discussion about fundamental attribution error and the inborn human tendency to overattribute the failings of others to their identities or groups. That's how *they* are . . .

The same phenomenon that allows us to so readily believe that smoking is the problem when there are clearly other explanations helps warp our perceptions of the members of other political tribes.

Researchers Douglas Ahler and Gaurav Sood explored the distance between perception and reality for their 2017 study "The Parties in Our Heads."[13] In an extensive survey, they asked Republicans and Democrats about themselves and about the members of their party. The gaps were jaw-dropping.

About 9 percent of Democrats said they were agnostics or atheists. Republicans guessed it was 36 percent. Republicans said that about 38 percent of Democrats were lesbian, bisexual, or gay. The real number was 6 percent. Republicans overstated the percentage of black Democrats by 22 points, and overshot on union membership by 33 points.

Democrats were closer in their perception of how southern and evangelical Republicans were, missing by 8 points and 10 points respectively. But Dems overshot bigly on two significant areas: They said 44 percent of Republicans had incomes of $250,000 or more. The real number was 6 percent. They also overestimated the share of Republicans who were age sixty-five or older by more than double the actual 21 percent.

It is appealing for cable news fans to imagine that supporters of the *other* brands are very different and inferior. In fact, the differences are negligible on most attributes. A 2018 *Wall Street Journal*/NBC News survey revealed that MSNBC viewers were a little older than Fox News viewers—only 19 percent of MSNBC viewers were between the ages of 35 and 49, compared to the 24 percent for Fox.[14]

Meanwhile, Fox's viewers were whiter, but not by a lot: 74 percent of Fox viewers were white, compared to 70 percent at MSNBC. The same for viewers' self-described socioeconomic status: An identical 44 percent of both groups described themselves as "middle class." Seventy percent of Fox viewers did not have college degrees, compared to 57 percent of MSNBC viewers, but other than that, a pretty similar demographic cohort. And yet, they often imagine one another as separate species.

Our culture war is taking place between imaginary armies, and because so many Americans live in politically homogeneous neighborhoods and consume siloed media, it's very hard for them to see reality.

That's why you have to learn to consume news skeptically, even from reliable outlets. I'm not talking about cynicism. I'm saying we should remember what David Hume wrote: "Reason is, and ought only to be the slave of the passions, and can never pretend to any other office than to serve and obey them."

Your wonderful mind is too good at rationalizing why the feelings you have are right. When you "trust your gut," it's really your brain that's working overtime—through, we hope, C. S. Lewis's "chest"—to make the case for doing or believing exactly what you want.

That's why, when a story about your political opponents or your own tribe lines up just perfectly with your assumptions, look out. That's when it's crucial to go back to the beginning and think about fundamental attribution error.

Are those people unemployed because they are smokers or are they unemployed for the same reasons that they smoke? Are your political opponents wrong because they are bad people, or do you *think* they are bad people because they are wrong in your eyes?

If you learn to start questioning your own assumptions when consuming news, you may learn to love your fellow Americans just a little more. You may come to see them as people like you. That could lead to mutual respect and goodwill. Who knows? Maybe even sometimes a politics of solutions, not performative outrage.

# ACKNOWLEDGMENTS

My deepest and most profound thanks go to my sons, Arthur and Newman. The Stirewalt brothers certainly aided in this endeavor by their ability to entertain themselves *quietly* over the course of many afternoons and evenings. But I could almost just as well thank the Sony Corporation for the invention of the PlayStation for that part. The boys' contribution went far beyond their sacrificial willingness to play *NHL '22* and *Hades*, though.

Watching them learn how to use and navigate the news media as adolescents has been invaluable to my thinking about the future of journalism and kept me away from a lot of fogeyism and false nostalgia. But most of all, they are my protections against cynicism and pessimism. For their sakes, I cannot afford to give in to despair about the intertwined fates of my vocation and our country. And because I see what bright, loving, decent, capable young men they are, it is easier to imagine a better future because they will be shaping it.

Speaking of young people who make you optimistic about the future, my research assistant at the American Enterprise Institute, the great Samantha Goldstein, has been indispensable at every step of this project. Her capacity for deep research and organization was a much-needed corrective to this crusty newsman's half-intelligible notes scribbled on envelope backs and left in voice mails to myself. Samantha was able to internalize the premise for this book when I could barely articulate it myself, and then she held me to it. Her questions and observations many times kept me from wandering off down the dark alleys and historical cul-de-sacs that I always find so appealing.

Samantha is the reason that *not once* do the names of those two *Washington Post* reporters played by Robert Redford and Dustin Hoffman in a movie appear in this book. Thanks to her gift for research, we were able to avoid the hackneyed narratives and historical examples that render so many books about the media into repetitive twaddle. My twaddle is *fresh*—based on new narratives and less-explored history and data. I may be wrong about a lot, but thanks to Samantha, I can be wrong in different and exciting ways. Plus, she was always up for working through lunch—especially when there was sushi involved.

She is in the right place, because as I have learned in my first year at AEI, it is truly a home for exceptional people. When our president, Robert Doar, and my boss, Yuval Levin, took me in after I became yet another casualty of post-journalism, I had no idea what to expect. What I found were not only the resources I needed to follow my passions, but something sorely lacking in many institutions today: the courage to defend free expression and free inquiry. At a time when we see the light going out in so many places, the leadership at AEI is holding the torch higher: a beacon, not a bunker. Thank God for them and the donors who make our work possible.

There are so many of my AEI colleagues whose work, advice, and encouragement have been precious to me, but I would be remiss if I did not mention Nicole Penn, Tim Carney, Matt Continetti, Andy Ferguson, Thomas Chatterton Williams, Kori Schake, Klon Kitchen, Jeffrey Rosen, Ryan Streeter, Michael

Strain, Ramesh Ponnuru, Sally Satel, Ajit Pai, Ed Pinto, Ben and Jenna Storey, and Adam White. In ways often unknown to them, they have enriched my work and made life far more delightful along the way. My colleagues John Fortier and Karlyn Bowman particularly have made me feel welcome and a part of a long, fine tradition. A special word for education scholar Robert Pondiscio, who reminded me what real literacy looks like, and why it's important to a free people.

What can I say about the mensch among mensches, Jonah Goldberg? No finer friend could a guy ask for. Many of the ideas in this book can be traced back to conversations with Jonah or ideas of his that I just plain stole. Through our years at Fox, during the turmoil that followed Fox shooting me out of a cannon, and still today, it is invaluable to have someone whom you can talk to about media and politics in conversations beginning with the phrase "Am I crazy, or . . . ?" He has found a way to balance the business and the journalism sides of our vocation in a most impressive fashion. His example as a father, journalist, and all-around human is a treasure.

What Jonah is building with my friend Steve Hayes at *The Dispatch* is a manifestation of the best aspirations in this book. When many in our business are giving up on fairness in favor of the easier path to profits through inciting hate and division, Steve and Jonah have made a big bet on decency, journalistic rigor, and constructive discourse. I am so proud to be an associate editor there and see my work alongside that of David French and the rest of our colleagues. Special thanks to Managing Editor Rachael Larimore, who indulged me in some *very* elastic deadlines as I worked on this book. It's a great crew, and one united in the belief that a significant market exists for real journalism if you give people a chance.

I'm grateful to my dear friend Eliana Johnson, with whom I get to do a journalism podcast, *Ink Stained Wretches*. I am so glad she pushed me out of my comfort zone to get into the messy work of media criticism. Every week, she teaches me something new, much of which can be found in the preceding pages. I joke that she is "the meanest person I like" when she takes the hide off some overstuffed member of the fourth estate, but in truth, she is lovely, generous, and kind. Just don't tell her I said so.

Thanks to the experts who agreed to be interviewed for this book: David Chavern, Rick Edmonds, and Dr. Gail Saltz. You were generous with your time and insights. Thanks also to Andrew Grant at the Pew Research Center, who accommodated our ever-deeper hunger for crosstabs.

My deep appreciation goes to Kathleen Morrison, PhD, assistant professor of behavioral neuroscience psychology at West Virginia University, for sharing her insights on constructivism and assimilation, without which this book would not have been possible.

I'm indebted to the great examples set by more journalists than I could possibly name, but I have to say a word about Hoppy Kercheval. He is a great broadcast journalist and writer, but while I just gas about the need for excellence, passion, and high standards on the local level, he is doing the work. The people of West Virginia don't know how lucky they are to have him.

I was supremely blessed in the selection of an editor for this book. Alex Pappas is an ink-stained wretch just like the rest of us, and I had the pleasure of working with him and becoming his friend when we were both at Fox News. While I am sorry that he left the news business, since we could surely use more like him, journalism's loss is my gain. Because he also came up in local news in a small state and then ran the rapids of national political coverage, Alex was the perfect partner in this endeavor. He is doing great things at Center Street and I couldn't be more pleased to be with him and his crew.

But then again, I have been amazingly lucky with editors in my career.

You heard quite a bit about Bill Sammon in this book, but I could have filled pages more. I called Bill "the skinny Buddha" for his capacity to keep cool under extraordinary stress, but his serenity is no joke. In a business where emotions run high and many mistakes are born of haste, Bill never forgot that our job was to get the story right every time. I watched him for years fight and win to maintain the standards at the Washington Bureau to allow great journalists to work freely there. His exit from Fox News was the harbinger of my imminent firing, but also more than that. It was the loss of a compass that pointed toward solid, ethical journalism even as pressure mounted to follow ratings wherever they would lead, even off a cliff.

I owe special thanks also to the greatest line editor in the history of the purple pen and a newsman of the highest order, Stephen G. Smith. Stephen had already been a grand vizier of national journalism at *Newsweek*, *Time*, and *U.S. News & World Report* before he took over the *Washington Examiner*. I have to assume it was desperation that led him to take a chance on me, a simple country pundit, for his politics editor, but I will take it. He probably had a soft spot for me because he too had worked in small markets before breaking into the big time. Stephen made me a better writer, showed me how the world of Washington media really works, and demonstrated daily an editor's duty to fight for his or her people. He set the bar high for us, but never higher than the one he set for himself. What I learned from him and Managing Editor Mike Hedges is worth two master's degrees in journalism, and was a lot more fun to do.

There have been many other great editors in my career, Jody Jividen, Dan Page, Nanya Friend, and Chris Stadelman among them, but Bob Kelly casts the longest shadow of them all. He was the guy who sized me up as a seventeen-year-old clueless kid and sent me back to learn the ropes as a sports reporter. I quickly came to idolize him for his cool, unflappable ways as well as his ability to laugh in the face of the deepest absurdities of small-market journalism. I followed in his footsteps to the *Charleston Daily Mail*, even on the same beats, even to become political editor. Every step of the way he was my advisor, partner in crime, and friend, something I have tried to be for the young reporters I have been privileged to work with.

Putting American journalism on a better path will not be achieved by sweeping changes or radical departures. It will be done by people like Bob applying steady pressure and calm resolve in the face of nitwit consultants, penny-pinching owners, outraged politicians, faddish journalism, shifting technology, and fickle consumers. They bend, but they don't break, and they keep getting the news out day after day. As he used to tell me when I was stuck on how to tackle a story, "Just write what you know."

# NOTES

## INTRODUCTION: AN ARGLE-BARGLE BUSINESS MODEL

1. Jaclyn Peiser, "A conservative cardinal who criticized the vaccine caught covid. Days later, he was put on a ventilator," *Washington Post*, September 16, 2021, https://www.washingtonpost.com/nation/2021/08/16/cardinal-raymond-burke-ventilator-covid/.

2. Claire Atkinson, "The Washington Post still plays catch-up, but is gaining on The Times," NBC News, December 28, 2017, https://www.nbcnews.com/news/us-news/washington-post-still-plays-catch-gaining-times-n833236.

3. James B. Stewart, "Washington Post, Breaking News, Is Also Breaking New Ground," *New York Times*, May 19, 2017, https://www.nytimes.com/2017/05/19/business/washington-post-digital-news.html.

4. Andrey Miroshnichenko, *Postjournalism and the Death of Newspapers: The Media after Trump: Manufacturing Anger and Polarization* (Toronto: Andrey Mir, 2020).

5. George Orwell, *Looking Back on the Spanish War* (London: New Road, 1943).

## CHAPTER 1. OUT OF IDEAS: HOW NEWS LOST A RACE TO THE BOTTOM WITH ITSELF

1. Robert Frost, "Stopping by Woods on a Snowy Evening," in *The Poetry of Robert Frost*, ed. Edward Connery Lathem (New York: Henry Holt, 1969).

2. E. D. Hirsch, "Cultural Literacy," *American Scholar* 52, no. 2 (1983): 159–69, http://www.jstor.org/stable/41211231.

3. Michael T. Nietzel, "Low Literacy Levels Among U.S. Adults Could Be Costing the Economy $2.2 Trillion a Year," *Forbes*, September 9, 2020, https://www.forbes.com/sites/michaeltnietzel/2020/09/09/low-literacy-levels-among-us-adults-could-be-costing-the-economy-22-trillion-a-year/?sh=75dbc04c4c90.

4. "The Drought," PBS, https://www.pbs.org/wgbh/americanexperience/features/dustbowl-drought/.

5. Greg Bradsher, "How the West Was Settled," *Prologue Magazine*, 2012, https://www.archives.gov/files/publications/prologue/2012/winter/homestead.pdf.

6. Donald A. Wilhite, "Dust Bowl," *The Encyclopedia of Oklahoma History and Culture*, https://www.okhistory.org/publications/enc/entry?entry=DU011.

7. Ellen Gray, "NASA Study Finds 1934 Had Worst Drought of Last Thousand Years," NASA Global Climate Change: Vital Signs of the Planet, October 15, 2014, https://climate.nasa.gov/news/2175/ nasa-study-finds-1934-had-worst-drought-of-last-thousand-years/.

8. "The Dust Bowl Suicides," KCTS9, https://www.kcts9.org/show/dust-bowl/clip/ dust-bowl-dust-bowl-suicides.

9. Caroline A. Henderson, "Letters from the Dust Bowl," *The Atlantic,* May 1936, https://www.theatlantic.com/magazine/archive/1936/05/ letters-from-the-dust-bowl/308897/.

10. "Black Sunday Remembered," Oklahoma Climatological Survey, April 13, 2010, http://climate.ok.gov/index.php/site/page/news/ black_sunday_remembered.

11. Ibid.

12. Ibid.

13. John H. Lienhard, "A Transatlantic Cable," Engines of Our Ingenuity, https:// www.uh.edu/engines/epi59.htm.

14. "The First News of House Business Submitted by Telegraph," United States House of Representatives: History, Art & Archives, May 25, 1844, https://history.house.gov/Historical-Highlights/1800-1850/ The-First-News-of-House-Business-Submitted-by-Telegraph/.

15. James Hamblin, "A Mapped History of Taking a Train Across the United States," *The Atlantic,* February 21, 2013, https://www.theatlantic.com/ technology/archive/2013/02/a-mapped-history-of-taking-a-train-across-the-united-states/266067/; "The First News of House Business Submitted by Telegraph," United States House of Representatives: History, Art & Archives. https://history.house.gov/Historical-Highlights/1800-1850/ The-First-News-of-House-Business-Submitted-by-Telegraph/.

16. "Veteran AP Reporter Turns 100," *Nevada Appeal,* January 25, 2003, https:// www.nevadaappeal.com/news/2003/jan/25/veteran-ap-reporter-turns-100/.

17. "Portfolio 2: Pictorial Journalism," Library of Congress, https://www.loc.gov/rr/ print/guide/port-2.html.

18. "Noyes Describes Wirephoto; Roses Parade Float Winners," *Star Tribune* (Minneapolis, MN), January 2, 1935, https://www.newspapers.com/ newspage/182966017/.

19. "Daily Times Second Newspaper in Iowa to Utilize Wirephotos," *Daily Times* (Davenport, IA), January 3, 1955, https://www.newspapers.com/clip/23731626/ wirephoto-can-transmit-photos-in-8/.

20. Nick Cataldo, "San Bernardino Hears of Lincoln's Death in 1865," *Sun* (San Bernardino, CA), July 24, 2017, https://www.sbsun.com/2015/04/27/ san-bernardino-hears-of-lincolns-death-in-1865/.

21. "A Transcontinental Telephone Line: July 1914," PBS, https://www.pbs.org/ transistor/background1/events/transcon.html.

NOTES

22. Susan R. Brooker-Gross, "News Wire Services in the Nineteenth-Century United States," *Journal of Historical Geography* 7, no. 2 (1981): 167–79, https:// doi.org/10.1016/0305-7488(81)90119-5.

23. Jesse Dukes, "Carl Sandburg's Chicago," WBEZ 91.5, https://interactive.wbez. org/curiouscity/sandburg-chicago/#at-work.

24. "William Cullen Bryant," Poetry Foundation, https://www.poetryfoundation. org/poets/william-cullen-bryant.

25. Joe Pompeo, "The Real Story of 'Headless Body in Topless Bar,' as Argued by Veterans of the 'Post,'" *Politico*, January 27, 2012, https://www.politico.com/ media/story/2012/01/the-real-story-of-headless-body-in-topless-bar-as-argued-by-veterans-of-the-post-000201/.

26. "Pennsylvania Gazette," Benjamin Franklin Historical Society, http://www. benjamin-franklin-history.org/pennsylvania-gazette/.

27. Ibid.

28. Kirsten Staples, "USPS Is Still a Great Option for Publishers," *Editor & Publisher*, January 27, 2022, https://www.editorandpublisher.com/stories/ usps-is-still-a-great-option-for-publishers,215220.

29. "Art1.S8.C7.1.1 Postal Power: Overview," Constitution Annotated, https:// constitution.congress.gov/browse/essay/artI-S8-C7-1-1/ALDE_00001068/.

30. Richard B. Kielbowicz, "The Press, Post Office, and Flow of News in the Early Republic," *Journal of the Early Republic* 3, no. 3 (Autumn 1983): 255–80.

31. Ibid.

32. "King's Highway," *South Carolina Encyclopedia*, https://www.scencyclopedia. org/sce/entries/kings-highway/.

33. James David Hart, *The Popular Book: A History of America's Literary Taste* (Berkeley: University of California Press, 1950).

34. Ibid.

35. Kielbowicz, "The Press, Post Office, and Flow of News in the Early Republic."

36. "James Madison to W. T. Barry," August 4, 1822, https://press-pubs.uchicago. edu/founders/documents/v1ch18s35.html.

37. "The Sedition Act of 1798," United States House of Representatives: History, Art & Archives, https://history.house.gov/Historical-Highlights/1700s/ The-Sedition-Act-of-1798/#:~:text=In%20one%20of%20the%20 first,government%20of%20the%20United%20States.

38. "Thomas Jefferson to James Currie, January 28, 1786," Library of Congress, https://www.loc.gov/resource/mtj1.005_0216_0218/?sp=1.

39. "Thomas Jefferson to John Norvell, June 11, 1807," Library of Congress, https:// www.loc.gov/resource/mtj1.038_0592_0594/?sp=1.

40. Robert M. S. McDonald, "Race, Sex, and Reputation: Thomas Jefferson and the Sally Hemings Story," *Southern Cultures* 4, no. 2 (Summer 1998): 46–63.

41. "American Newspapers, 1800–1860: City Newspapers," University of Illinois Library, https://www.library.illinois.edu/hpnl/tutorials/ antebellum-newspapers-city/.

42. Robert Frost, "A Servant to Servants," 1915, https://www.bartleby.com/118/9. html.

43. Stephen Smith, "Radio: The Internet of the 1930s," APM Reports, November 10, 2014, https://www.apmreports.org/episode/2014/11/10/ radio-the-internet-of-the-1930s.

44. Ibid.

45. U.S. Census Bureau, "Historical Households Tables," November 2021, https:// www.census.gov/data/tables/time-series/demo/families/households.html.

46. Smith, "Radio: The Internet of the 1930s."

47. Huey Long, "Every Man a King," NBC, February 23, 1934, http://www. emersonkent.com/speeches/every_man_a_king.htm.

48. Robert E. Snyder, "Huey Long and the Presidential Election of 1936," *Louisiana History: The Journal of the Louisiana Historical Association* 16, no. 2 (1975): 117–43, https://www.jstor.org/stable/4231456.

49. Elizabeth Kolbert, "The Big Sleazy," *The New Yorker*, June 4, 2006, https:// www.newyorker.com/magazine/2006/06/12/the-big-sleazy.

50. Edward F. Haas, "Huey Long and the Dictators," *Louisiana History: The Journal of the Louisiana Historical Association* 47, no. 2 (2006): 133–51, https://www. jstor.org/stable/4234177.

51. "Reverend Charles E. Coughlin (1891–1979)," PBS, https://www.pbs.org/ wgbh/americanexperience/features/holocaust-coughlin/.

52. Thomas Doherty, "The Deplatforming of Father Coughlin," *Slate*, January 21, 2021, https://slate.com/technology/2021/01/father-coughlin-deplatforming-radio-social-media.html.

53. Ibid.

54. Tianyi Wang, "Media, Pulpit, and Populist Persuasion: Evidence from Father Coughlin," *American Economic Review* 111, no. 9 (September 2021): 3064–92, https://www.aeaweb.org/articles?id=10.1257/aer.20200513.

55. "A Veteran Editor Gone," *New York Times*, November 26, 1886, https:// timesmachine.nytimes.com/timesmachine/1886/11/26/103127995.pdf.

56. Jack Shafer, "How the Byline Beast Was Born," Reuters, July 6, 2012, https://web.archive.org/web/20120707071407/http://blogs.reuters.com/ jackshafer/2012/07/06/how-the-byline-beast-was-born/.

57. "Scenes from Hell," National Archives, https://www.archives.gov/exhibits/ eyewitness/html.php?section=5.

58. Martin P. Wattenberg, *Is Voting for Young People?* (Taylor & Francis, 2020).

59. Ibid.

60. William G. Mayer, "Trends in Media Usage," *Public Opinion Quarterly* 57, no. 4 (Winter 1993): 593–611, https://doi.org/10.1086/269398.

61. Wattenberg, *Is Voting for Young People?*

## CHAPTER 2. TURNING THE TELESCOPE AROUND: HOW MEDIA DISRUPTION DISORDERED NEWS JUDGMENT

1. Lee Ross, "The Intuitive Psychologist and His Shortcomings: Distortions in the Attribution Process," *Advances in Experimental Social Psychology* 10 (1977): 173–220, https://doi.org/10.1016/S0065-2601(08)60357-3.

2. Neil Munro, "Obama Uses Coffee Cup to Salute Marines," *Daily Caller*, September 23, 2014, https://dailycaller.com/2014/09/23/obama-uses-coffee-cup-to-salute-marines/.

3. "Editorial: Barack Takes a Bow," *Washington Times*, April 7, 2009, https://www.washingtontimes.com/news/2009/apr/07/barack-takes-a-bow/#ixzz2zoIZiqNS.

4. Michelle Malkin, "Video: Obama's Deep Bow to the Saudi King," *Unz Review*, April 2, 2009, https://www.unz.com/author/michelle-malkin//2009/04/02/video-obamas-deep-bow-to-the-saudi-king/.

5. "Obama's Bow in Japan Sparks Some Criticism," NBC News, November 16, 2009, https://www.nbcnews.com/id/wbna33978533.

6. Matt Wilstein, "Once 'Shocked' by Obama's 'Latte Salute,' Hannity Ignores Trump Saluting North Korean General," *Daily Beast*, June 14, 2018, https://www.thedailybeast.com/once-shocked-by-obamas-latte-salute-hannity-ignores-trump-saluting-north-korean-general.

7. Rebecca Morin, "Trump Faces Backlash after Saluting North Korean General," *Politico*, June 14, 2018, https://www.politico.eu/article/donald-trump-north-korea-general-faces-backlash-after-saluting/.

8. Robert P. Vallone, Lee Ross, and Mark R. Lepper, "The Hostile Media Phenomenon: Biased Perception and Perceptions of Media Bias in Coverage of the Beirut Massacre," *Journal of Personality and Social Psychology* 49, no. 3 (1985): 577–85, https://doi.org/10.1037//0022-3514.49.3.577.

9. Russell J. Dalton, Paul A. Beck, and Robert Huckfeldt, "Partisan Cues and the Media: Information Flows in the 1992 Presidential Election," *American Political Science Review* 92, no. 1 (1998): 111–26, https://doi.org/10.2307/2585932; Cindy T. Christen, Prathana Kannaovakun, and Albert C. Gunther, "Hostile Media Perceptions: Partisan Assessments of Press and Public during the 1997 United Parcel Service Strike," *Political Communication* 19, no. 4 (2002): 423–36, https://doi.org/10.1080/10584600290109988; Stephanie Jean Tsang, "Empathy and the Hostile Media Phenomenon," *Journal of Communication* 68, no. 4 (2018): 809–29, https://doi.org/10.1093/joc/jqy031; Laura M. Arpan and Arthur A. Raney, "An Experimental Investigation of News Source and the Hostile Media Effect," *Journalism and Mass Communication Quarterly* 80, no. 2 (2003): 265–81, https://doi.org/10.1177/107769900308000203.

10. "Immigration," Gallup, July 27, 2021, https://news.gallup.com/poll/1660/immigration.aspx.

11. "News Media," Kansas City Area Development Council, https://thinkkc.com/life/entertainment/news-media.

12. Katerina Eva Matsa and Jacob Liedke, "Local TV News Fact Sheet," Pew Research Center, July 13, 2021, https://www.pewresearch.org/journalism/fact-sheet/local-tv-news/.

13. Ibid.

14. Georg Szalai, "TV Station Giants to Benefit from Record Political Ads in 2020, Analyst Says," *Hollywood Reporter*, September 9, 2020, https://www.hollywoodreporter.com/news/general-news/tv-station-giants-to-benefit-from-record-political-ads-in-2020-analyst-says-4057114/.

15. Howard Homonoff, "2020 Political Ad Spending Exploded: Did It Work?" *Forbes*, December 8, 2020, https://www.forbes.com/sites/howardhomonoff/2020/12/08/2020-political-ad-spending-exploded-did-it-work/?sh=3056d86e3ce0.

16. Ibid.

17. Matsa and Liedke, "Local TV News Fact Sheet."

18. Ibid.

19. Penelope Muse Abernathy, "The News Landscape in 2020: Transformed and Diminished," University of North Carolina Hussman School of Journalism and Media, June 22, 2020, https://www.usnewsdeserts.com/reports/news-deserts-and-ghost-newspapers-will-local-news-survive/the-news-landscape-in-2020-transformed-and-diminished/.

20. David Strömberg and James M. Snyder Jr., "Press Coverage and Political Accountability," *Journal of Political Economy* 118, no. 2 (2010): 355–408, https://doi.org/10.1086/652903.

21. Sam Schulhofer-Wohl and Miguel Garrido, "Do Newspapers Matter? Short-Run and Long-Run Evidence from the Closure of *The Cincinnati Post*," *Journal of Media Economics* 26 (2013): 60–81, https://doi.org/10.1080/08997764.2013.785553.

22. Matthew Gentzkow, Jesse M. Shapiro, and Michael Sinkinson, "The Effect of Newspaper Entry and Exit on Electoral Politics," *American Economic Review* 101, no. 7 (2011): 2980–3018, https://www.aeaweb.org/articles?id=10.1257%2Faer.101.7.2980; Danny Hayes and Jennifer L. Lawless, "The Decline of Local News and Its Effects: New Evidence from Longitudinal Data," *Journal of Politics* 80, no. 1 (2018): 332–36, https://www.journals.uchicago.edu/doi/10.1086/694105; Marion R. Just, "Nothing to Read: Newspapers and Elections in a Social Experiment," *American Political Science Review* 90, no. 4 (1996): 918–19, https://doi.org/10.2307/2945885.

23. Pengjie Gao, Chang Lee, and Dermot Murphy, "Financing Dies in Darkness? The Impact of Newspaper Closures on Public Finance," Brookings Institution, no. 44 (2018): 1–39, https://www.brookings.edu/wp-content/uploads/2018/09/WP44.pdf.

24. U.S. Census Bureau, "Pulaski County, Missouri," 2021, https://www.census.gov/quickfacts/fact/table/US/PST045221.

25. "Missouri State Auditor's Office County Budget Package," State of Missouri, Pulaski County, 2020, https://nebula.wsimg.

com/0edde439b6effc919cbc9140c64e9a3d?AccessKeyId=
95893235017642B81EBB&disposition=0&alloworigin=1.

26. David Bauder and David A. Lieb, "Decline in Readers, Ads Leads Hundreds of Newspapers to Fold," Associated Press, March 11, 2019, https://apnews.com/ article/north-america-waynesville-mo-state-wire-us-news-newspapers-0c59cf4a09114238af55fe18e32bc454.

27. Steven D. Levitt and John A. List, "Was There Really a Hawthorne Effect at the Hawthorne Plant? An Analysis of the Original Illumination Experiments," National Bureau of Economic Research, no. 15016 (2009): 1–19, https://doi.org/10.3386/w15016.

28. Rob McCarney et al., "The Hawthorne Effect: A Randomised, Controlled Trial," *BMC Medical Research Methodology* 7, no. 30 (2007), https://doi.org/10.1186/1471-2288-7-30.

## CHAPTER 3. BUBBLE TROUBLE: HOW THE NEWS BUSINESS LOST CONTACT WITH THE REAL WORLD

1. "Victims of Intentional Homicide: 2018," United Nations Office on Drugs and Crime, https://dataunodc.un.org/content/homicide-rate-option-2.

2. Hans J. G. Hassel, John B. Holbein, and Matthew R. Miles, "There Is No Liberal Media Bias in Which News Stories Political Journalists Choose to Cover," *ScienceAdvances* 6, no. 14 (2020), https://www.science.org/doi/10.1126/sciadv.aay9344.

3. Ibid.

4. Tim Groseclose and Jeffrey Milyo, "A Measure of Media Bias," *Quarterly Journal of Economics* 120, no. 4 (2005): 1191–1237, https://doi.org/10.1162/003355305775097542.

5. "American Views 2020: Trust, Media and Democracy," Knight Foundation, August 4, 2020, https://knightfoundation.org/reports/american-views-2020-trust-media-and-democracy/.

6. Andrew McGill, "U.S. Media's Real Elitism Problem," *The Atlantic*, November 21, 2016, https://www.theatlantic.com/politics/archive/2016/11/fixing-americas-nearsighted-press-corps/508088/.

7. Ibid.

8. Tucker Doherty and Jack Shafer, "The Media Bubble Is Real—and Worse than You Think," *Politico Magazine*, 2017, https://www.politico.com/magazine/story/2017/04/25/media-bubble-real-journalism-jobs-east-coast-215048/.

9. Haya El Nasser, "More than Half of U.S. Population in 4.6 Percent of Counties," U.S. Census Bureau, October 24, 2017, https://www.census.gov/library/stories/2017/10/big-and-small-counties.html.

10. Elizabeth Grieco, "Newsroom Employees Are Less Diverse than U.S. Workers Overall," Pew Research Center, November 2, 2018, https://www.pewresearch.org/fact-tank/2018/11/02/newsroom-employees-are-less-diverse-than-u-s-workers-overall/.

11. "The 2019 U.S. Energy and Employment Report," National Association of State Energy Officials and Energy Futures Initiative, 2019, https://www.usenergyjobs.org/2019-report.

12. Jim Rutenberg, "Trump Is Testing the Norms of Objectivity in Journalism," *New York Times*, August 7, 2016, https://www.nytimes.com/2016/08/08/business/balance-fairness-and-a-proudly-provocative-presidential-candidate.html.

13. Public Religion Research Institute/*The Atlantic* Mid–October 2016 Survey, October 11, 2016, https://www.prri.org/wp-content/uploads/2016/10/PRRIThe-Atlantic-Survey-Topline-Oct.-9.pdf; NBC News/*Wall Street Journal* Mid October Poll, October 13, 2016, https://www.scribd.com/document/327796832/16991-NBCWSJ-Mid-October-Poll.

14. Batya Ungar-Sargon, *Bad News: How Woke Media Is Undermining Democracy* (New York: Encounter Books, 2021).

15. U.S. Census Bureau, Current Population Survey (CPS), Annual Social and Economic Supplement, "Rates of high school completion and bachelor's degree attainment among persons age 25 and over, by race/ethnicity and sex," National Center for Education Statistics, 2015, https://nces.ed.gov/programs/digest/d15/tables/dt15_104.10.asp.

16. Ibid.

17. U.S. Census Bureau, American Community Survey Public Use Microdata, "Educational Attainment for Workers 25 Years and Older by Detailed Occupation," Employment Projections Program, 2021, https://www.bls.gov/emp/tables/educational-attainment.htm.

## CHAPTER 4. WEAK PARTIES, STRONG PARTISANSHIP: HOW THE SILOED MEDIA HURTS DEMOCRATS AND REPUBLICANS

1. George C. Kohn, *The New Encyclopedia of American Scandal* (New York: Facts on File, 2021), 168.

2. Robert Mitchell, "The first midterm 'wave' election that ended total Republican control of government," *Washington Post*, November 4, 2018, https://www.washingtonpost.com/history/2018/11/04/midterm-wave-election-that-set-standard-them-all/.

3. Katie Rodgers and Iliana Maraga, "Trump Stuns Grieving Britons: Meet the Suspect in Your Son's Death," *New York Times*, February 4, 2021, https://www.nytimes.com/2019/10/16/world/europe/donald-trump-harry-dunn-anne-sacoolas.html.

4. Ali Vitali, "Trump Floats Pay Bonus for Teachers Who Carry Guns in Class," NBC News, February 22, 2018, https://www.nbcnews.com/politics/white-house/trump-floats-bonuses-teachers-willing-carry-guns-class-n850281.

5. Michael Sykes, "Trump Floats Season Suspension for NFL Players Protesting Anthem," Axios, July 20, 2018, https://www.axios.com/trump-nfl-national-anthem-policy-miami-dolphins-eaad5167-1ee8-4e21-b04c-061d642c000d.html.

6. Ibid.

7. Gregory Korte, "Trump Blasts 'Treasonous' Democrats for Not Applauding at his State of the Union Address," *USA Today*, February 5, 2018, https://www.usatoday.com/story/news/politics/2018/02/05/trump-blasts-treasonous-democrats-not-applauding-his-state-union-address/301962002/.

8. Hope Yen and Calvin Woodward, "AP Fact Check: Trump's Takes on Impeachment, Syria, Climate," Associated Press, October 26, 2019, https://apnews.com/article/ap-fact-check-health-donald-trump-syria-ap-top-news-610ad7eb58ad4a85a50f5adc61418 02d.

9. "Airport Traffic Report," Port Authority of New York and New Jersey, 2020, https://www.panynj.gov/content/dam/airports/statistics/statistics-general-info/annual-atr/ATR_2020.pdf.

10. Alexander Sammon, "Ikea's Race for the Last of Europe's Old-Growth Forest," *New Republic*, February 16, 2022, https://newrepublic.com/article/165245/ikea-romania-europe-old-growth-forest.

11. Michael Powell, "Once a Bastion of Free Speech, the A.C.L.U. Faces an Identity Crisis," *New York Times*, September 28, 2021, https://www.nytimes.com/2021/06/06/us/aclu-free-speech.html.

12. Timothy Noah, "Hey, Larry David, Your Super Bowl Commercial Was Pretty, Pretty, Pretty Bad," *New Republic*, February 15, 2022, https://newrepublic.com/article/165376/larry-david-crypto-super-bowl-commercial-pretty-pretty-pretty-bad.

13. Abigail Tracy, "'If You Aren't Making News, You Aren't Governing': Matt Gaetz on Media Mastery, Influence Peddling, and Dating in Trump's Swap," *Vanity Fair*, September 14, 2020, https://www.vanityfair.com/news/2020/09/matt-gaetz-donald-trump-firebrand.

14. Yuval Levin, *A Time to Build* (New York: Basic Books, 2020), 48.

15. Ibid, 48–49.

16. Peri E. Arnold, "William Taft: Campaigns and Elections," University of Virginia Miller Center, https://millercenter.org/president/taft/campaigns-and-elections.

17. Stephen Stagner, "The Recall of Judicial Decisions and the Due Process Debate," *American Journal of Legal History* 24, no. 3 (1980): 257–72, https://doi.org/10.2307/844667.

18. "How FDR Lost His Brief War on the Supreme Court," National Constitution Center, February 5, 2022, https://constitutioncenter.org/blog/how-fdr-lost-his-brief-war-on-the-supreme-court-2.

19. "John N. Garner (1933–1941)," University of Virginia Miller Center, https://millercenter.org/president/fdroosevelt/essays/garner-1933-vicepresident.

20. Anne Dingus, "John Nance Garner," *Texas Monthly*, November 1996, https://www.texasmonthly.com/news-politics/john-nance-garner/.

21. Dave Helling, "1944 Democratic Convention: Choosing Not Just a VP Candidate but a President-in-Waiting," *Kansas City Star*, July 18, 2016, https://www.kansascity.com/news/politics-government/election/article88007192.html.

22. Elizabeth Grieco, "Americans' Main Sources for Political News Vary by Party and Age," Pew Research Center, April 1, 2020, https://www.pewresearch.org/fact-tank/2020/04/01/americans-main-sources-for-political-news-vary-by-party-and-age/.

23. Greg Gutfeld, *The Joy of Hate: How to Triumph over Whiners in the Age of Phony Outrage* (New York: Crown Forum, 2014).

24. Jonathan Weisman and Reid J. Epstein, "G.O.P. Declares Jan. 6 Attack 'Legitimate Political Discourse,'" *New York Times*, February 4, 2022, https://www.nytimes.com/2022/02/04/us/politics/republicans-jan-6-cheney-censure.html.

25. Melissa Bell, "Richard Nixon and Roger Ailes 1970s Plan to Put the GOP on TV," *Washington Post*, July 1, 2011, https://www.washingtonpost.com/blogs/blogpost/post/richard-nixon-and-roger-ailes-1970s-plan-to-put-the-gop-on-tv/2011/07/01/AG1W7XtH_blog.html.

## CHAPTER 5. OUTSOURCING OUR MORALITY: HOW PERSONALITY-DRIVEN COVERAGE LEADS TO NIHILISM

1. Sarah Kaplan, "Climate change has destabilized the Earth's poles, putting the rest of the planet in peril," *Washington Post*, December 14, 2021, https://www.washingtonpost.com/climate-environment/2021/12/14/climate-change-arctic-antarctic-poles/.

2. Jacqueline Alemany and Mariana Alfaro, "House Jan. 6 committee votes to hold Meadows in contempt, details texts from Trump allies who wanted him to call off rioters," *Washington Post*, December 13, 2021, https://www.washingtonpost.com/politics/jan-6-house-meadows-subpoena/2021/12/13/271713a6-5c1d-11ec-bda6-25c1f558dd09_story.html; Jada Yuan, "Discovering Dr. Wu," *Washington Post*, December 13, 2021, https://www.washingtonpost.com/lifestyle/2021/12/13/chien-shiung-wu-biography-physics-grandmother/.

3. Tik Root, "From novelist to climate crusader: How one woman is working to put a stop to natural gas," *Washington Post*, September 30, 2021, https://www.washingtonpost.com/climate-solutions/interactive/2021/change-natural-gas-audrey-schulman/?utm_source=ourcommunitynow&utm_medium=web; Danny Funt, "Pets can help fight climate change with an insect-based diet. Owners just need to come around to the idea," *Washington Post*, September 21, 2021, https://www.washingtonpost.com/climate-solutions/2021/09/21/pet-food-sustainable-bugs-insects/; Darryl Fears, "A harvest for the world: A Black family farm is fighting racism in agriculture and climate change," *Washington Post*, June 28, 2021, https://www.washingtonpost.com/climate-environment/climate-solutions/interactive/2021/harvest-world-black-family-farm-is-fighting-racism-agriculture-climate-change/.

4. Andrea Petersen, "More People Are Taking Drugs for Anxiety and Insomnia, and Doctors Are Worried," *Wall Street Journal*, May 25, 2020, https://www.

wsj.com/articles/more-people-are-taking-drugs-for-anxiety-and-insomnia-and-doctors-are-worried-11590411600.

5. Sam Stein (@samstein), "A lot to process on the Manchin news but, from a substantive standpoint, it's just objectively devastating for the planet. The last best chance at climate change legislation is gone," Twitter, December 19, 2021, https://twitter.com/samstein/status/1472576562142887948?lang=en.

6. Logan Reardon, "Who Are the Highest Paid Coaches in the NFL This Season?" NBC Sports, October 14, 2021, https://www.nbcsports.com/boston/patriots/who-are-highest-paid-coaches-nfl-2021-season.

7. "Judiciary Hearing Erupts as Mazie Hirono Tells Ted Cruz to Stop 'Mansplaining,'" YouTube, *The Hill*, June 23, 2021, https://www.youtube.com/watch?v=S9gYtmBHNVA.

8. Nicholas Confessore and Karen Yourish, "$2 Billion Worth of Free Media for Donald Trump," *New York Times*, March 15, 2016, https://www.nytimes.com/2016/03/16/upshot/measuring-donald-trumps-mammoth-advantage-in-free-media.html.

9. Theodore Schleifer, "Trump on Carson: 'Better Off If You Stab Someone?'" CNN, November 9, 2015, https://www.cnn.com/2015/11/09/politics/donald-trump-ben-carson-allegations/index.html.

10. Dylan Byers, "Can Bloomberg Buy 2016?" *Politico*, May 5, 2014, https://www.politico.com/blogs/media/2014/05/can-bloomberg-buy-2016-187968.

11. Jason Zengerle, "Joe Scarborough Has Big Dreams (Including 'Trump: The Musical')," *GQ*, September 18, 2016, https://www.gq.com/story/joe-scarborough-has-big-dreams-trump-musical.

12. Jason Linkins, "Michael Bloomberg Sure Paid a Lot for This Zamboni Ride." *HuffPost*, November 3, 2015, https://www.huffpost.com/entry/michael-bloomberg-donald-trump_n_56385cdde4b027f9b969ebe9.

13. Eliza Collins, "Les Moonves: Trump's Run Is 'Damn Good for CBS,'" *Politico*, February 29, 2016, https://www.politico.com/blogs/on-media/2016/02/les-moonves-trump-cbs-220001.

14. Ibid.

15. Dylan Byers, "Fox News Will Be 'Loyal Opposition' to Biden, Fox CEO Says," NBC News, March 4, 2021, https://www.nbcnews.com/media/fox-news-will-loyal-opposition-biden-fox-ceo-says-rcna355.

16. John Bowden, "Trump: I Will Win 2020 Because 'Media Will Tank' Without Me," *The Hill*, December 28, 2017, https://thehill.com/homenews/campaign/366742-trump-i-will-win-in-2020-because-media-will-tank-without-me.

17. Joseph Choi, "News Networks See Major Viewership Drop in 2021," *The Hill*, December 27, 2021, https://thehill.com/homenews/media/587401-news-networks-see-major-viewership-drop-in-2021.

18. Ibid.

19. "Transcript: Ezra Klein Interviews Chris Hayes," *New York Times*, January 11, 2022, https://www.nytimes.com/2022/01/11/podcasts/transcript-ezra-klein-interviews-chris-hayes.html.

## CHAPTER 6. POST-JOURNALISM OR ASPIRATIONAL FAIRNESS? HOW TO BUILD A BETTER NEWS BUSINESS

1. Andrey Miroshnichenko, *Postjournalism and the Death of newspapers: The Media after Trump: Manufacturing Anger and Polarization* (Toronto: Andrey Mir, 2020).

2. Andrey Miroshnichenko, "Postjournalism: From the world-as-it-is to the world-as-it-should-be," Human as Media, November 11, 2020, https://human-as-media.com/2020/11/11/postjournalism-from-the-world-as-it-is-to-the-world-as-it-should-be/.

3. George Orwell, *Looking Back on the Spanish War* (1943).

4. Nikole Hannah-Jones, *The 1619 Project: A New Origin Story* (United States: One World, 2021).

5. Arun Venugopal, "'1619 Project' Journalist Says Black People Shouldn't Be an Asterisk in U.S. History," NPR, November 17, 2021, https://www.npr.org/2021/11/17/1056404654/nikole-hannah-jones-1619-project.

6. Jake Silverstein, "We Respond to the Historians Who Critiqued the 1619 Project," *New York Times Magazine*, December 20, 2019, https://www.nytimes.com/2019/12/20/magazine/we-respond-to-the-historians-who-critiqued-the-1619-project.html.

7. Wesley Morris, "Why Is Everyone Always Stealing Black Music?" *New York Times Magazine*, August 14, 2019, https://www.nytimes.com/interactive/2019/08/14/magazine/music-black-culture-appropriation.html.

8. Hannah-Jones, *The 1619 Project*.

9. Caleb Ecarma, "Tucker Carlson Goes Full 1/6 Truther in New Fox Doc," *Vanity Fair*, October 28, 2021, https://www.vanityfair.com/news/2021/10/tucker-carlson-january-6-truther.

10. "The 1619 Project: A New Origin Story Hardcover," Amazon, https://www.amazon.com/1619-Project-New-Origin-Story/dp/0593230574.

11. *Fox Nation*, https://nation.foxnews.com/.

12. Andrey Miroshnichenko, "Postjournalism: From the world-as-it-is to the world-as-it-should-be."

13. "Veteran AP Reporter Turns 100," *Nevada Appeal*, January 25, 2003, https://www.nevadaappeal.com/news/2003/jan/25/veteran-ap-reporter-turns-100/.

14. G. Greeley Wells, "The Man Who Carried the Flag at Iwo Jima," *New York Times*, October 17, 1991, https://www.nytimes.com/1991/10/17/opinion/l-the-man-who-carried-the-flag-at-iwo-jima-631591.html.

15. Jill Colvin, "Russia Conflict Separates GOP Traditionalists from Newcomers," Associated Press, February 24, 2022, https://apnews.

com/article/russia-ukraine-joe-biden-jd-vance-vladimir-putin-russia-
58ad695dd865df38b390d6e830bf38a1.

16. Jane Mayer, "The Big Money Behind the Big Lie," *The New Yorker*,
August 2, 2021, https://www.newyorker.com/magazine/2021/08/09/
the-big-money-behind-the-big-lie.

17. Holly Otterbein, "Squad Member to Deliver Response to Biden SOTU,"
*Politico*, February 23, 2022, https://www.politico.com/news/2022/02/23/
squad-member-to-deliver-response-to-biden-sotu-00010877.

18. Glenn Greenwald, "The Pressure Campaign on Spotify to Remove Joe Rogan
Reveals the Religion of Liberals: Censorship," Glenn Greenwald on Substack,
January 29, 2022, https://greenwald.substack.com/p/the-pressure-campaign-
on-spotify?utm_source=substack&utm_campaign=post_embed&utm_
medium=email.

19. Taylor Dysart, "The Ottawa Trucker Convoy Is Rooted in Canada's
Settler Colonial History," *Washington Post,* February 11, 2022, https://
www.washingtonpost.com/outlook/2022/02/11/ottawa-trucker-convoy-is-
rooted-canadas-settler-colonial-history/; Sohrab Ahmari, "Against David
French-ism," First Things, May 29, 2019, https://www.firstthings.com/
web-exclusives/2019/05/against-david-french-ism.

20. Rutenberg, "Trump Is Testing the Norms of Objectivity in Journalism."

21. Tracy, "'If You Aren't Making News, You Aren't Governing.'"

22. George Orwell, *The Front of Your Nose* (London: Tribune, 1946).

23. Ben Smith, "Brandon Just Wants to Drive His Racecar," *New York Times*,
December 19, 2021, https://www.nytimes.com/2021/12/19/business/brandon-
brown-lets-go-brandon.html.

24. Ibid.

25. Chris Stirewalt and Eliana Johnson, "*Ink Stained Wretches*, the Interview:
Ben Smith," January 6, 2022, in *Ink Stained Wretches*, produced by Nebulous
Media, podcast, MP3 audio, 53:41, https://www.aei.org/multimedia/
ink-stained-wretches-the-interview-ben-smith/.

26. Mallory Mower, "32 Products That'll Make You Think 'Wow, This is a Need,'"
BuzzFeed, February 11, 2022, https://www.buzzfeed.com/malloryannp/
products-thatll-make-you-think-wow-this-is-a-need?origin=hpp.

27. "Local Measurement: Methodology," Nielsen, March 27, 2016, https://
web.archive.org/web/20160327180124/http://en-us.nielsen.com/sitelets/cls/
documents/nielsen/Local-Measurement-Methodology-Ex.pdf.

28. "2017 Nielsen DMA Rankings—2017 Television Season," Lyons Public
Relations Broadcast PR Solutions, January 18, 2017, https://www.lyonspr.com/
latest-nielsen-dma-rankings/.

29. "Negative Tone Ramps Up as Gov Primary Nears in W.Va.," *Herald-Dispatch*
(Huntington, WV), May 10, 2011, https://www.herald-dispatch.com/news/
negative-tone-ramps-up-as-gov-primary-nears-in-w-va/article_668a5e9a-9806-
5117-af4b-1fb4c4a41775.html.

30. Lauren Feiner and Alex Sherman, "Politico Sells to German Publishing Giant Axel Springer in Deal Worth about $1 billion," CNBC, August 26, 2021, https://www.cnbc.com/2021/08/26/axel-springer-to-buy-politico.html.

## CHAPTER 7. AN INSIDE JOB: HOW TO LIVE A BETTER LIFE AND MAKE A BETTER COUNTRY THROUGH NEWS JUDGMENT

1. Stephenie Overman and Kate Andrews, "Reagan National's $660M Expansion Nearly Ready for Takeoff," Virginia Business, October 27, 2020, https://www.virginiabusiness.com/article/46697/.

2. Charles Murray, *Coming Apart: The State of White America, 1960–2010* (New York: Crown Forum, 2013).

3. "Ipsos Understanding Society: Wave 1 April 2021," Ipsos (Cornell University, Ithaca, NY: Roper Center for Public Opinion Research, 2021), https://ropercenter.cornell.edu/ipoll/study/31118527.

4. Alexis C. Madrigal, "When Did TV Watching Peak?" *The Atlantic*, May 30, 2018, https://www.theatlantic.com/technology/archive/2018/05/when-did-tv-watching-peak/561464/.

5. Lee Rainie, "Cable and Satellite TV Use Has Dropped Dramatically in U.S. since 2015," Pew Research Center, March 17, 2021, https://www.pewresearch.org/fact-tank/2021/03/17/cable-and-satellite-tv-use-has-dropped-dramatically-in-the-u-s-since-2015/.

6. Mason Walker and Katerina Eva Matsa, "News Consumption Across Social Media in 2021," Pew Research Center, September 20, 2021, https://www.pewresearch.org/journalism/2021/09/20/news-consumption-across-social-media-in-2021/.

7. Michael Barthel et al., "Measuring News Consumption in a Digital Era," Pew Research Center, December 8, 2020, https://www.pewresearch.org/journalism/2020/12/08/measuring-news-consumption-in-a-digital-era/.

8. Rudy Takala, "GOP Sen. Cramer Demands Fox Fire Chris Stirewalt and Other 'Knuckleheads' for Arizona Call: They Owe the 'American People an Apology,'" Mediaite, November 6, 2020, https://www.mediaite.com/news/gop-sen-cramer-demands-fox-fire-chris-stirewalt-and-other-knuckleheads-for-arizona-call-they-owe-the-american-people-an-apology/.

9. Flora Lewis, "Foreign Affairs; Worthwhile Canadian Initiative," *New York Times*, April 10, 1986, https://www.nytimes.com/1986/04/10/opinion/foreign-affairs-worthwhile-canadian-initiative.html.

10. Neal Rothschild and Sara Fischer, "America Can't Quit Polarizing Politicians," Axios, January 29, 2022, https://www.axios.com/polarizing-politicians-cruz-aoc-03e1b0b5-0748-48c7-a576-a32ff83d5361.html.

11. Jennie Dusheck, "Smokers Have Harder Time Getting Jobs, Study Finds," Stanford Medicine, April 11, 2016, https://med.stanford.edu/news/all-news/2016/04/smokers-have-harder-time-getting-jobs-study-finds.html.

12. "Current Cigarette Smoking Among Adults in the United States," Centers for Disease Control and Prevention, December 10, 2020, https://www.cdc.gov/tobacco/data_statistics/fact_sheets/adult_data/cig_smoking/index.htm.

13. Douglas J. Ahler and Gaurav Sood, "The Parties in Our Heads: Misperceptions About Party Composition and Their Consequences," *Journal of Politics* 80, no. 3 (July 2018), https://doi.org/10.1086/697253.

14. Bill McInturff, "Who's Watching? A Look at the Demographics of Cable News Channel Watchers," Public Opinion Strategies, February 1, 2019, https://pos.org/whos-watching-a-look-at-the-demographics-of-cable-news-channel-watchers/.

# ABOUT THE AUTHOR

CHRIS STIREWALT is a political columnist, author, and former political editor of the Fox News Channel, where he served on the election night Decision Desk, helped coordinate political coverage across the network, and frequently provided on-air analysis. He is a senior fellow at the American Enterprise Institute, where he focuses on American politics, public opinion, and the media. He is a contributing editor and weekly columnist for *The Dispatch* and cohosts a media criticism podcast, *Ink Stained Wretches*. He is the author of *Every Man a King: A Short, Colorful History of American Populists* (Twelve Books, 2018), in which he looks at American populism through the lives of seven famous populists.